Interpreting Protestantism to Catholics

Interpreting Protestantism to Catholics

by

WALTER R. CLYDE

Philadelphia

THE WESTMINSTER PRESS

PRINTED IN THE UNITED STATES OF AMERICA

Clyde, Walter R

Interpreting Protestantism to Catholics. Philadelphia, Westminster Press [1959]

160 p. 21 cm.

1. Protestant churches — Relations — Catholic Church. 2. Catholic Church — Relations — Protestant churches. I. Title.

BX4817.C57 284 59-5624‡

Library of Congress

Contents

A First Word

This book is an attempt to explain Protestantism to Catholics so that Catholics can better understand Protestantism and Protestants, and in the explanation, it is hoped, that Protestant readers may see their own faith in a new light.

A distinguished Catholic professor, the Rev. John A. O'Brien, Ph.D., of the University of Notre Dame, wrote an article for the magazine *Look,* February 21, 1956, in which he stressed the need for Protestants, Catholics, and Jews to live together in greater good will. He remarked that one of the major sources of conflict among them was their lack of accurate information about each other. Then he suggested as his first remedy: "Have the members of the different faiths know one another personally as well as understand their respective creeds. Ignorance born of isolation is the breeding ground of suspicion and prejudice, which, as its etymology (pre+judge) indicates, means a passing of judgment before the facts are known."

Surely Father O'Brien is right. American Protestants, Catholics, and Jews do need to know how to live together in greater good will. And to do that they do need to escape the ignorance born of isolation from each other. They need to communicate with each other, to talk with each other, and thereby to learn each other's distinctive religious viewpoints.

This book would contribute to the Catholic-Protestant phase of that desirable interfaith communication. It would help Catholics understand what Protestants believe by explaining to them something of Protestant life and thought. The explanation is not complete. But, the author hopes, it will provide Catholics with the essentials of Protestantism; and it introduces the Protestant position on two matters that raise numerous domestic and community problems between Catholics and Protestants — marriage and education.

This explanation of Protestantism seeks to be an explanation only, not an argument for Protestantism and against Catholicism. Often, it will be seen, Protestant and Catholic views are compared with each other, and the Protestant judgment about Catholic views given. But this is not done to support Protestantism or to oppose Catholicism. It is done to help Catholics see just how the Protestant understanding of Christianity differs from their own. Also, it is done to help Protestant readers see how Protestant and Catholic views compare so that they can better explain Protestantism to Catholic friends.

Finally, the author would pay tribute to two Catholic friends, a husband and wife. He writes his explanation of Protestantism with genuine appreciation for the profundities of Catholic thought and the splendors of Catholic life. In a large measure his appreciation has been inspired by the friendship his wife and he enjoy with the Catholic couple. The couple's devotion to their Catholicism, joined with their tolerance and appreciation shown in so many ways to the author's Protestantism, has meant much to him. It has helped him to grow in tolerance and appreciation for their Catholicism while he remains faithful to his own Protestantism.

W. R. C.

CHAPTER I | *The Fact of Protestantism*

When American Catholics put a name to Protestants as a religious group, they often refer to them, not as Protestants, but as non-Catholics. Catholics do this quite properly. Protestants as a religious group standing apart from the Roman Catholic Church can be included with all other groups standing apart from the Roman Catholic Church for religious reasons, such as Jews, Orthodox Catholics, Hindus, and Moslems. But Protestants also have a religious character of their own, and in that character they constitute a large, widely distributed, and influential part of the world's religious population in general and of the world's Christian population in particular.

I

It is estimated that among the world's almost three billion people there are about 850,000,000 Christians. These Christians divide into three major groups: Roman Catholics, with about 400,000,000 adherents; the Orthodox and Eastern Catholics, with about 175,000,000; and the Protestants, with 225,000,000. According to percentages, of the total number of Christians in the world, 50 per cent are Roman Catholics and almost 28 per cent are Protestants.

Protestants, along with Roman Catholics, are to be found as minority groups in the many countries dominated by non-Christian religions. Thus, for example, China has about 1,500,000 Protestants and 3,000,000 Catholics; India about 4,500,000 Protestants and 3,000,000 Catholics; and in Africa there are many millions of both Protestant and Catholic Negro converts. This is the result of the extensive missionary work of European and American Protestants and Catholics.

In some parts of the world Protestants outnumber Roman Catholics. That is true generally in the northern countries of Europe, including England and excluding Russia. And it is true in the United States, where other religious groups are relatively very small. To give exact Protestant and Catholic population figures for the United States is impossible since most Protestant churches count only their adult membership while the Roman Catholic Church counts both its baptized infants and its baptized adults. But the approximate figures are 35,000,000 adult Protestants and 18,000,000 adult Roman Catholics, or about two adult Protestants for every adult Roman Catholic.

The comparative number of Protestants and Catholics in the United States is obscured by the fact that their distribution across the country is uneven. Catholics are in the majority in most of the major Northern cities and smaller industrial communities, in the Southwest, and in occasional " pockets " in the rural Midwest. Protestants are in the majority in the suburbs of the cities, in the South, and through most of the rural areas.

This uneven distribution is largely the result of immigration. The early migrants to what is now the United States were mostly Protestants who came from Protestant areas of Europe, England, Scotland, the Netherlands, Sweden, and from the Protestant sections of Germany. Exceptions were Catholics from Spain who entered the Southwest by way of Mexico. Otherwise, Protestants settled everywhere. From about 1850 on, however, large numbers of Catholics came from Catholic areas of Europe, Ireland, Italy, the Balkans, and from the Catholic sections of Germany. In recent years many Catholics have come from Quebec, in Canada, and from Puerto Rico, where Catholics are greatly in the majority. Mostly the Catholics settled in the area close to their ports of entry — the Northeast; in the places where they could get work — the cities and the industrial communities; and only occasionally where a group of them had means and opportunity to buy land — in the Midwest rural " pockets."

Protestants are found throughout the world, not simply as Protestants, but also as Protestants belonging to different denominations, or separate organizations. The major denominations are the Anglican or Episcopalian, Baptist, Lutheran, Methodist, and Presbyterian. In addition there are a great number of other denominations.

In the United States the denominational existence of Protestantism is readily apparent to Catholics who see about them the church buildings of different Protestant denominations. There are about two hundred Protestant denominations. Most Protestants, however, are concentrated in a few of them. Ninety-five per cent of American Protestants belong to the twenty largest denominations, and 85 per cent belong to the ten largest denominations.

So large and so widely distributed a number of Protestants makes them highly influential in the world at large and, especially, in the United States. And when that is combined with the vigor of Protestant life and thought, Protestants become one of the most influential elements in world and national experience. Their influence is felt in education, art, science, philosophy, politics, and in men's special religious effort to know God and to live with him.

So far as the United States is concerned, throughout most of its history the majority position of Protestants has made them the most influential religious group. Whether they remain that today, or whether Catholics equal them or surpass them in influence, is not important here. What is important is the fact that Protestants, along with Catholics, constitute by far the two most influential religious groups in contemporary American life.

II

Protestants who live in the same world and the same nation with Catholics are like Catholics in calling themselves Christians. This they do, of course, on the basis of their idea of what Christians are. Catholics, on the other hand, have their own idea of what Christians are. Consequently Catholics must decide whether Protestants, in claiming to be Christians, do so legitimately.

As Protestants see it, Christians are those who commit their lives to Jesus Christ as the supreme revelation of God. For Christians to make such commitment means that they seek to believe and to do what Jesus Christ wants them to believe and to do because they see in him what God is like, what God does to meet men's needs, what God wants men to do. Christians thus commit themselves to God because they see in Jesus Christ the very presence of God himself. Accordingly, as Christians they do not consider themselves to be simply the followers of a man; much more, they commit themselves to be the followers of God incarnate, or truly present, in Jesus Christ.

Protestants, then, consider themselves to be Christians when they commit themselves to Jesus Christ. Catholics devoutly call Jesus Christ, " Our Lord." They call him " Our Lord " because by committing their lives to him, to believe what he would have them to believe and to do what he would have them to do, they make him the Lord, or the Ruler, of their lives. And they call him " Our Lord," with a capital " L," because they do not commit their lives to a mere man, but to God himself. For them, God has come to earth in Jesus Christ; for them, God is in heaven in Jesus Christ; for them, Jesus Christ is the divine Lord to whom they pledge the absolute loyalty of their souls.

It is of significance for Catholics that Protestants judge

Catholics to be Christians on the same basis that Protestants judge themselves to be Christians. Not long ago, in the spring of 1957, the Protestant minister, Dr. Billy Graham, held a series of religious services in New York City's Madison Square Garden. He invited the thousands who attended to commit themselves to Jesus Christ, and to sign cards on which they would indicate churches to which his executive committee might refer them. Dr. Graham was asked what he thought about a Catholic's signing a card, and referring the Catholic to a Catholic church. A newspaper reported him as answering that he would refer the Catholic to a Catholic church, and as going on to say: " After all, I have no quarrel with the Catholic Church. Christians are not limited to any church. The only question is: Are you committed to Christ? "

This expresses the conviction of most Protestants about the Christianity of Catholics: Catholics are Christians if they are committed to Jesus Christ. It is necessary to make the qualification that "most Protestants" hold this conviction because, unfortunately, not all Protestants hold it. Some Protestants, a very few of them, refuse to grant that any Catholic can be a Christian. But most Protestants, in saying that Catholics are Christians if they are committed to Jesus Christ, rejoice in believing that Catholics can be and often are just as genuinely Christians as Protestants can be.

But what do Catholics think of the claim of Protestants to be Christians? Do Catholics agree that Protestants, through commitment of their lives to Christ, can legitimately make that claim? Informed Protestants must confess that many Protestants are quite mistaken about the Catholic position on this question. Many Protestants think that the Catholic Church holds what it certainly does not hold — that Protestants cannot be Christians, and so all Protestants are doomed to hell.

It is true, of course, that sometimes even Catholics talk

that way. A few years ago a small group of Boston Catholics claimed that only Roman Catholics are saved. Their bishop was unable to change their minds. At last he took the most drastic action possible, action intended not only to punish the group but to demonstrate to all that they did not speak the mind of the Catholic Church. He excommunicated them.

Catholic doctrine certainly requires all men to belong to the Catholic Church to be saved. But men can belong to the Catholic Church and be saved without becoming Catholics in the strict sense. Indeed, both Protestants and pagans can belong to the Catholic Church and be saved without being regular members of it.

First of all, it is necessary that the non-Catholics live in invincible ignorance, not in vincible ignorance. Invincible ignorance is ignorance for which they are not responsible, the ignorance in which, for some good reason, they do not realize that they ought to join the Catholic Church. Vincible ignorance is ignorance for which they are responsible, the ignorance in which, although they know that they ought to join the Catholic Church, they refuse to do so.

Non-Catholics living in invincible ignorance can become members of the soul of the church, a status contrasting with that of Catholics who are members of the body of the church, or the visible church. Protestants become members of the soul of the church through Protestant baptism, provided they are baptized in the name of the Trinity. Pagans become members of the soul of the church when once in their lives they perform a perfect act of contrition, an act in which they truly confess their sins and seek God's forgiveness and salvation. And as long as both Protestants and pagans continue in invincible ignorance and commit no mortal sin, they are saved.

Protestants, then, in calling themselves Christians, can often do so with considerable legitimacy where Catholics are concerned. Indeed, as Roman Catholics see it, a great many Protestants are truly Christians because they belong to the soul of the Catholic Church. Accordingly, Catholics recognize that in living in the same world and in the same nation with Protestants they do not live altogether with pagans. They live with many Protestants who are as truly Christian as they are.

Of course, there are good and bad Protestants; there are faithful and unfaithful Protestants; there are practicing and nonpracticing Protestants; there are loyal and lapsed Protestants. Catholics can discover representations of both types. It is important, however, for Catholics to recognize that the existence of good, faithful, practicing, loyal Protestants means that Protestantism is not another name for indifferentism in religion.

There is a tendency among Catholics to equate Protestantism with indifferentism, to think that Protestants do not take Christianity very seriously. A Catholic priest observes in a book of *Instructions for Non-Catholics before Marriage:* " It is true that non-Catholics, for the most part, give very little thought to religion, and so for them it matters little what religion they profess." And just before this comment the priest mentions Lutherans and Episcopalians, who are Protestants.

Unfortunately, there is considerable justification for this attitude. In the first years when American young men were being drafted for World War II, a group of young men were overheard discussing an Army examination they had just taken. One said: " It asked what religion. I didn't know what to put down." Another replied, " Do you eat fish on Friday? " The first young man said, " No." And promptly came the answer, " Well, then you're a Protestant! "

Some Protestants are not much as Protestants; and Catholics can point to a good deal of evidence to prove the point. There are the Protestants who attend church only spasmodically, if at all. There are some Protestants who marry Catholics and are quite content to have their children raised as Catholics. And there are those who exhibit their Protestantism only at their death — when their funeral service is conducted by a Protestant clergyman.

But Catholics can understand that such Protestants do not equate Protestantism with indifferentism any more than do similar Catholics equate Catholicism with indifferentism. Catholicism too has its bad representatives — its unfaithful, and nonpracticing, and lapsed Catholics. And the evidence is similar to that cited concerning poor Protestants. There are the Catholics who attend church only spasmodically, if at all; the Catholics who marry Protestants and allow their children to be raised as Protestants; the Catholics who exhibit their Catholicism only at the time of death — when they seek the last rites of the Catholic Church.

It is fruitless to debate whether there are more poor Protestants or more poor Catholics, or whether Protestants or Catholics are more faithless to their particular religious profession. The situation varies in different parts of the United States and in different areas of the world; and the factors at work are sociological as well as religious. Among sociological factors, for example, is the fact that Protestants and Catholics, like other groups, often tend to be more devoted to their principles when they are only a minority in the community. Here one can compare the few and zealous Protestants in Catholic South America with the few and zealous Catholics in Protestant Scotland. It is enough to point out that the world has both its poor Protestants and its poor Catholics.

And, correspondingly, it is enough to point out that along with good Catholics, there are good Protestants. There are Protestants who let no Sunday go by without going to church to worship. There are many who decline to marry Catholics because they want their children to be educated as Protestants. Certainly Protestants are not necessarily careless Christians, and Protestantism is not another name for religious indifferentism.

For that reason, active Protestants are often somewhat

sensitive about the application to them of the term "non-Catholic." It has already been observed that there is no doubt about the correctness of the term. Since Protestants are not Catholics, they are non-Catholics, and can be so called to distinguish them from Catholics. But, rightly or wrongly, Protestants sometimes feel that Catholics, in referring to Protestants as non-Catholics, often include the idea that Protestants stand for little, that they are non-Catholics whose religious position at best is negative.

Active Protestants, however, do stand for much. They hold convictions valid to their minds, determinative to their wills, and dear to their hearts. Theirs is a positive religious position, and they like to think that this is expressed in the term "Protestant." "Protestant" comes from the Latin words *pro,* meaning "for," and *testari,* meaning "to testify." Hence, active Protestants are people who testify or bear witness to something. They testify or bear witness to the particular understanding of Christian faith and life that active Protestants affirm with all their heart.

Protestants would suggest that Roman Catholics, when seeking to learn more about Protestants, ought not to neglect the study of Protestants at their best. It has just been admitted: not all Protestants are good Protestants. This admission includes both the fact that not all Protestants are faithful Protestants and the fact that not all are informed Protestants. Not all Protestants are fully representative of Protestantism in their life and thought. If, then, Roman Catholics concentrate their attention upon such Protestants as true representatives of Protestant life and thought, they study only caricatures of what Protestants and Protestantism really are. Certainly such a procedure, by not dealing with the best representatives of Protestantism, at the least is inadequate, and at the most is scarcely sensible and fair.

Unfortunately Protestants often do the same sort of thing where Roman Catholics are concerned: they study only the poorest representatives of Catholic Christianity and conclude that these individuals exhibit what Catholics and Catholicism really are. A Catholic chaplain attached to an American Army unit in a Catholic Caribbean country was addressed by a new Protestant acquaintance who wanted to express a friendly attitude: "I suppose you're glad to be down here among so many Catholics." And the Catholic chaplain exclaimed, "Don't call these people Catholics!" He meant that the ignorant Catholic people of the country, so ignorant and superstitious and even careless of their religious obligations, were scarcely Catholics at all. Yet Protestants sometimes point out such Catholics and say, "Here is what Catholics and Catholicism really are." To do this is for Protestants to draw conclusions from caricatures of Catholics and Catholicism. Whenever they do, they are not sensible and fair and owe Catholics their apologies.

This is not to say, of course, that Catholics ought never to study the poorest representatives of Protestantism. After all, caricatures have their value. They exaggerate distinctive or peculiar characteristics of their subjects, and though the result is grotesque and not altogether fair, it renders these characteristics unmistakable. For example, the intensely individualistic Protestant is not the best Protestant; the best Protestant has strong elements of individualism balanced by strong elements of co-operativeness. But the intensely individualistic Protestant does, as a kind of caricature, strikingly exhibit the fact that strong elements of individualism are peculiarly characteristic of Protestantism.

Still, Catholics should study the finest Protestants if they would discover what Protestantism really is. Through such Protestants they see Protestantism accurately represented, not distorted by exaggerations of particular parts, but with all parts in proper balance. Only thus can Catholics make accurate and fair appraisals of Protestantism.

CHAPTER II | *Common Elements*

Father Thurston N. Davis is a Jesuit and editor in chief of the excellent Jesuit weekly *America*. Back in March, 1957, Father Davis wrote in his paper: "Protestants and Catholics should get together to talk over — not merely their differences — the vast areas of common concern that they have. I think that Catholics should take the initiative." Father Davis is right. Catholics and Protestants do have vast areas of common concern. If they did not, neither could lay claim to the name "Christian," nor would they want to. And certainly, holding so many things in common, they should recognize the fact and try increasingly to discover what their elements of likeness are.

I

When Catholics do what Father Davis suggests — seek out their areas of agreement with Protestants — they are often surprised to find that Protestants are one with them in so many things. An elderly Catholic lady and her husband attended the Protestant funeral of a Protestant niece. The lady was an Italian American who had come to the United States as a young girl, and who had lived a restricted life of hard work and family devotion that had allowed her few opportunities for education and acquaintance with life around her. Her attendance at the Protestant funeral was her first experience of Protestant worship. Afterward she spoke appreciatively to the Protestant pastor who had conducted the funeral service. " Why," she said, " it wasn't so different! You said what we believe — about the resurrection. And you said the ' Our Father ' — though of course there was a little more at the end of it." This fine Catholic lady, to her surprise, had found that Protestants hold elements of belief familiar to her. The Lord's Prayer was said in the longer Protestant form, the form with the final doxology, " For thine is the kingdom and the power and the glory, forever." Still, unmistakably, it was what the Catholics call it, the " Our Father."

And, Catholics will be interested to know, the Protestant Lord's Prayer is becoming even more like the Catholic " Our Father." The traditional and common Protestant version of the Lord's Prayer comes from an old Protestant translation of the Bible, the King James Version, made in England back in 1611. The King James Version has the doxology at the conclusion of the Lord's Prayer. But recent Protestant translations of the New Testament omit the doxology, since it is not to be found in the earliest copies of the New Testament. The most widely used recent Protestant translation of the Bible is the Revised Standard Version, which was completed in 1952. It is, incidentally, the version from which the Scripture passages in this book are taken. The Revised Standard Version drops the doxology of the Lord's Prayer from its main text and places it in a footnote with the comment that it is added by " other authorities, some ancient . . ." In the main text of the Revised Standard Version, the Lord's Prayer then reads like the " Our Father."

Catholics most sense their kinship with Protestants when Protestants and Catholics face a common enemy, when they face an enemy opposed not just to Catholics or to Protestants but to all who claim to be Christians. So it was that in the days of Hitler's Germany, when the Nazis sought to cripple the Christian church, whether Catholic or Protestant, the Catholics and Protestants fought back together. They went to prisons and concentration camps; and in prisons and the concentration camps together they prayed and died. To some extent, faced by a foe that would destroy them both, they were driven together simply to survive. But their experience went deeper than that. Faced by an anti-Christian foe, Catholics and Protestants knew themselves to be Christians together.

Today Catholics often recognize this as they find themselves one with Protestants in opposing anti-Christian communism. A Protestant minister on a Sunday conducted morning services in a town some miles distant from his own. Starting to drive home, he passed a family of four, the parents and two small children, waiting for a bus. The weather was hot; the minister knew they would have some time to wait until a bus came; so he stopped and offered them a ride. They responded gratefully, and the minister drove them almost to their destination. During the conversation en route, he introduced himself to them as a Protestant minister who had just been conducting church services. " Oh," the husband and father exclaimed, " that's fine! We're Catholics. But just so we're opposed to communism together." Certainly many thoughtful Catholics, and Protestants too, would consider this comment somewhat superficial. But the Catholic who made it was not trying to be profound. He was speaking simply in a neighborly spirit with a Protestant; and in that spirit he expressed his recognition that Catholics and Protestants, confronted by anti-Christian communism, are linked together as Christians. And this remains true however differently Protestants and Catholics may feel that communism should be opposed.

But Catholics need no enemy common to themselves and Protestants to recognize their " vast areas of common concern " with Protestantism. These areas they can discover at any time by simple observation of Protestant faith and practice. To assist Catholics in doing this, some of the things Protestants as Christians believe and practice along with Catholics will now be pointed out.

II

Imagine a Catholic who knows nothing about Protestants. He has lived only with other Catholics. He does not even know that Protestants exist! Then one day he moves away from his fellow Catholics and without knowing it finds himself among Protestants. He wants to discover what religion his new neighbors follow, so he begins to observe their religious practices. He would find their religious practices very similar to his Catholic practices, so similar that for a while he would suppose them to be Catholics like himself.

He would find their religious practices centering around buildings much like the buildings around which Catholic religious practices center. From the outside he would see that the buildings had steeples and stained-glass windows. From the inside he would see that each building had a main large room equipped with pews, pulpits, and an organ. And he would see, used outside and inside in numerous locations and ways, a cross.

Inside some of these buildings he would see, at the front of their main large rooms, an arrangement almost identical with the altars at the front of his Catholic church; in other buildings he would see a pulpit that would make him think of the pulpits in Catholic churches, and a Bible that would make him think of the Bible in Catholic churches. He would be able to see the pictures and symbols in the stained-glass windows. Many of them he would recognize as identical with pictures and symbols in the stained-glass windows of Catholic churches, such as a picture of Christ healing the sick, a symbol of a crown with a cross in it.

He would see the people of the area gathered in these main large rooms, doing in them some of the same things that Catholics do when they gather in their churches to worship: they would pray, listen to a man who stands in the pulpit and talks, give an offering, sing hymns. In fact, were he to leaf through the hymnbook from which they sing, he would recognize some of the authors of the hymns as being Catholic, and some of the hymns as being the same hymns sung in Catholic churches. Eventually, he would observe the people celebrating, in their own fashion, but unmistakably, two of the Catholic sacraments, Baptism and Holy Communion.

He would see that the men speaking from the different pulpits bore similarities to Catholic priests. Some of them wore vestments; all of them talked about Jesus Christ, from whom men learn about God and whom men ought to follow. If he went into the studies or offices of these men, he would see on their bookshelves books by great doctors of the Catholic Church, like Augustine and Thomas Aquinas. He might even see an entire set of the writings of the apostolic fathers. Eventually, he would see these men going to visit people in need, and officiating at marriages and funerals.

He would observe the people leave the large main rooms in their buildings. He would see them acting much as Catholics do in the regular routine of life's activities, trying to be like the man Jesus Christ, failing often, but trying. He would see them dealing kindly with their families, helping the poor, building schools and hospitals, striving for good and struggling against evil.

He would see all these and many more things similar to Catholic practices; and at the beginning he might think himself among some kind of Catholics, especially if he knew that Catholic practices vary in different countries. In fact, knowing no more about these people than has been suggested, he might even enter their buildings with them, to pray, to sing, and to listen with them to their speaker. He might be able to worship with them, particularly after he heard them call themselves " Christians," and after he heard them call their buildings and association together "churches." He would feel, from all this that he observed, that there was a likeness between their attitude toward God and his Catholic attitude toward God. And he might be surprised to learn, after a while, that they were not Catholics, but a religious group new to him — Protestants.

Protestants may suggest that Catholics would do well to give attention to the similarities among Catholic and Protestant religious practices just observed. Catholics can easily ignore these similarities or be unimpressed by them; for American Catholics, unlike our hypothetical Catholic, know from the outset that Protestants constitute a religious group separate from Catholics, with characteristics of its own. But the similarities among Catholic and Protestant religious practices are there; and Catholics attending to them can thereby be reminded that Protestants are a religious group not totally dissimilar from themselves.

III

At the same time, American Catholics can find among Protestants religious similarities that lie deeper than the more or less external similarities just pointed out, and also similarities in belief and attitude that comprise essential elements in the theological structure of both Catholicism and Protestantism. These concern such matters as the nature of the world, the existence and nature of God, the nature of men, the importance of Jesus Christ, the significance of the church, the manner of the Christian life, and the ultimate destiny of men. At these points Catholics can often hear Protestants voicing convictions similar to their own.

Protestants, like Catholics, take a spiritual view of the world. They believe, for one thing, that the ultimate reality of the world is not material: it is not the sort of thing that can be sensed physically, measured, weighed, computed, or described as an electrical particle. The ultimate reality of the world is spiritual: it is the reality of which God is composed, and of which, by God's design, men's souls are composed. Also, in their spiritual view of the world, Protestants believe that the ultimate reality of the world has an existence superior to that of the material elements of the world. Thus God in the final degree, and men in a lesser degree, are masters of the material elements; and thus God and men cannot be the victims of the death or the disintegration of the material elements. Still further, in their spiritual view of the world, Protestants believe that mysteries exist beyond the comprehension of men. Men participate only partly in the ultimate, spiritual reality of the world. In the fullest sense, the ultimate, spiritual reality of the world is divine, or God. And this means that men can never fully comprehend the mystery of God's being and purpose.

Protestants, like Catholics, believe in a God who is personal, creative, providential, good, and just. Being personal, God thinks, sets objectives, wills, and feels; he is not a mere set of values, or natural laws, or cosmic stuff. Because he is creative, God has made the universe and all within it; the universe has no existence from eternity and apart from him. As providential, God upholds and controls the universe and all within it; the universe is not self-sustaining, and it cannot resist God who orders it as he pleases. Since he is good, God is the source of goodness, truth, and beauty; the universe receives all these positive elements from him. And since he is just, God resists evil and condemns it; the evils in the universe God wars against and ultimately conquers.

Protestants and Catholics alike believe that God makes himself known to men. He has done this in the past; he does it today. On the one hand, God makes himself known to men by giving evidence of himself. This evidence is given, in general, in the " goods " of the universe, such as the orderliness and beauty of nature, and the wisdom and virtue of men. God gives evidence of himself, in a particular way, in the Bible, which in its Old Testament is the record of his special revelation through the Hebrew people, and which in its New Testament is the record of that revelation through Jesus Christ. On the other hand, God makes himself known to men by giving them the ability to examine this evidence. He gives men such ability, in general, in the basic intellectual capacities possessed by all men and, in particular, in the special powers of understanding that he grants to Christian men.

Both Protestants and Catholics believe that men are under God's judgment as God's sinful children. In his goodness God, who creates men as spiritual beings like himself, looks upon them as his children. As God's children, men are bound to obey God. And men can obey him. For men created by God are not animals or the helpless victims of the evil forces of the universe; they are personalities free to choose to obey or to disobey God. Unfortunately, they choose to disobey him and thereby become his sinful children. As God's sinful children, men are judged by God. God recognizes them to be guilty of disobedience toward him. Consequently, he brings upon them a variety of earthly misfortunes; and he separates them from himself, in this life and in the life to come — an experience that for men is hell.

Protestants, like Catholics, believe that God saves men from their sin and its effects through his incarnation in Jesus Christ. In Jesus Christ, who lived two thousand years ago, God lived; God became man in Jesus Christ. Jesus Christ was God working in love and power to save men from the source and the consequences of their sins. In thus saving men, Jesus Christ lived a perfect life, died upon the cross, was resurrected from the dead, and ascended into heaven. In his life, death, resurrection, and ascension, Jesus Christ brought men the love and power of God. By God's love men receive forgiveness for their sins, such release from earthly misfortunes as he sees fit, and, in any case, strength to endure those which come. By God's power men turn from disobeying to obeying God. And by God's gracious provision men who are saved are brought to the joyous experience of heaven.

The belief that God works through the Holy Spirit is common to Protestants and Catholics. Here Protestants, along with Catholics, extend their conception of God to what is known in Christian theology as the Trinitarian view of God. In some fashion beyond men's ability fully to understand, the one God exists in a complex way experienced by men in three forms. There is God the Father as he is experienced by men generally; there is God the Son as he is experienced by men through his incarnation in Jesus Christ; there is God the Holy Spirit as he is experienced within men whenever he gives them inward guidance. The Holy Spirit, therefore, is God at work within men to guide them in particular ways in thought and deed. And where terminology is concerned, the Holy Spirit as God so working can also be called the Holy Spirit of God. God is God, but as a complex being he expresses himself in an aspect that is his Son and in an aspect that is his Holy Spirit.

Protestants, like Catholics, believe that God has made the followers of Jesus Christ to be a special community, that is, the church. God calls men to follow Jesus Christ, and as men respond to that call God makes them into a company of those who believe, worship, and live according to his will as he declares it in Jesus Christ. God thus causes the church to exist in the world as the fellowship of the saints, or the brotherhood of those who have answered his call in Christ. Moreover, the church exists in the world as the body of Christ. The Christ once present in the earth is now in heaven, but through his followers who constitute the church he continues to speak and act in the earth.

Protestants share with Catholics the belief that God calls

upon men to obey the Ten Commandments and Christ's teachings, spirit, and example. This means, specifically, things like the following. It means that Christians should seek to relieve suffering and to preserve life; that Christians should be kindly, honest, and peaceful in their dealings with all men, and that they should respect the sanctity of marriage and the rights of children. It also means that they should do to others as they want others to do to them. All these things and more, Christians should do to carry out the Ten Commandments and the guidance of Jesus Christ in their ordinary lives.

Protestants, like Catholics, believe in the continuing existence of men beyond death to such a destiny as God intends for them. Earthly existence is not men's only existence. Death is not the final curtain in the drama of life. It signals but an interlude between the earthly acts of the drama of life and the eternal acts of the drama of life yet to be played. God grants men a life beyond this life. What that future life will be like for particular men God determines according to the character of their relations with him. If God finds them to be his sinful children, the provision he makes for them is an unhappy one. If they are his obedient children, the provision he makes for them is a happy one.

Through these Protestant beliefs Catholics can gain some idea of the convictions Protestants hold in common with them. These beliefs only suggest how extensively Protestants and Catholics agree. Actually, Protestants and Catholics can talk for hours, or write whole series of books, on their agreements without once disagreeing. It could not be otherwise since they both, Catholics and Protestants, trace their heritage back to the same Bible and the same Christ as revelations of the same God.

Indeed, Protestant churches generally also trace their heritage back to great creedal statements of Christian belief that are authorities in the Roman Catholic Church:

the Apostles' Creed and the Nicene Creed. These Protestant churches place the two creeds among their own doctrinal standards, or fundamental beliefs. Besides, they often repeat the ringing affirmations of the Apostles' Creed in their services of public worship:

> "I believe in God the Father Almighty, Maker of heaven and earth;
> "And in Jesus Christ his only Son our Lord; who was conceived by the Holy Ghost, born of the Virgin Mary, suffered under Pontius Pilate, was crucified, dead, and buried; he descended into hell; the third day he rose again from the dead; he ascended into heaven, and sitteth on the right hand of God the Father Almighty; from thence he shall come to judge the quick and the dead.
> "I believe in the Holy Ghost; the holy catholic church; the communion of saints; the forgiveness of sins; the resurrection of the body; and the life everlasting. Amen."

To be sure, Catholics may object that Protestants make their own distinctive interpretations of the creeds. But the fact that Protestants accept and use the creeds shows how much they are one with Catholics on basic Christian convictions. Protestants do not live in a thought world entirely apart from Catholics; they live in one where they live, in many respects, with Catholics. So American Protestants and Catholics living in the same geographical and cultural area do not live entirely apart from each other in the area of Christian belief and life. In a multitude of ways they live together.

IV

Of course, despite the agreements with Catholics in so many ways, Protestants remain Protestants. They not only interpret points of agreement in their own ways, but on other points they are frankly and sincerely in disagreement with Catholics. That is why they are Protestants, why such a book as this can be written, and why the rest of the book will be saying so much about them.

But if Catholics and Protestants keep remembering that they have "vast areas of common concern," it will help them understand each other in several ways. They can find in them points of contact through which they converse and work with each other. And they can experience a sense of brotherhood as they know themselves bound together by common beliefs and ideals, and common hopes and aspirations.

CHAPTER III | *The Bible*

This chapter begins the description of the distinctively Protestant understanding of Christianity; and it concerns what Protestants believe about the Bible. As has been observed, Protestants, like Catholics, believe that God makes himself known throughout the Bible. But beyond that Protestants have views of their own about the Bible that largely determine everything else they say about Christianity.

Suppose two men go to a Catholic and a Protestant, asking how they can learn about Christianity. The one man is a non-Christian who wants to become a Christian; the other man is a Christian who wants to become a better Christian. They go first to the Catholic. The Catholic tells them: "To learn about Christianity seek out the Catholic Church. The Catholic Church can teach you without fail what God has revealed in the Bible and in apostolic tradition." Then they go to the Protestant. He tells them: "To learn about Christianity search the Bible. The Bible can teach you without fail what God has revealed."

This imagined incident, similar to many incidents that actually occur, points out the distinctive Protestant view about the basis of Christian experience, or about how men become Christians and grow as Christians. Whereas Catholics find the basis for Christian experience in the teachings of the Catholic Church, Protestants find it in the Bible. In doing so, Protestants no more ignore the church than

Catholics ignore the Bible. But while Catholics look to the Catholic Church as the teacher of the Bible, Protestants look to the Bible itself. For Protestants, the Bible itself is the primary basis of Christian experience because the Bible itself is the primary source of Christian knowledge.

This, then, is distinctive about Protestants as soon as they begin to describe Christianity as they see it: they are people of a book, and that book is the Bible. For Protestants, the Bible is fundamental to Christian experience. They begin with the Bible to learn how to be Christians, and they continue with the Bible to learn how to be better Christians. Numerous Protestant practices illustrate this. Protestants buy so many Bibles that they make the Bible a perennial best seller. Protestant Bible societies concentrate upon the translation, printing, and distribution of the Bible. There is at least one Bible in almost every Protestant home. Bibles are commonly given to their children by Protestant parents and churches. Protestants study the Bible in all sorts of classes and schools, and they write and publish about the Bible a tremendous number of books of all types and for all ages.

Since Protestants do make so much of the Bible, an explanation of their distinctive understanding of Christianity can well start by describing their view of the Bible. The present chapter does this in four parts.

I

First, Protestants believe that the Bible is the infallible and authoritative Word of God.

Both Protestants and Catholics call the Bible the infallible and authoritative Word of God, and they do so for the same reason. Both believe that God presents himself to the men of each generation infallibly — as he actually is; he presents himself to them authoritatively — they must accept him as he is. In so doing, God presents himself to them through words that make him known —

the words of the Bible. Hence all the words of the Bible, taken together, comprise the Word of God, or the means by which God presents himself to men. Thus far Protestants and Catholics agree. But then they begin to differ on how God presents himself to men through the Bible and on how men receive him.

For Catholics, God presents himself by giving in the Bible a body of infallible and authoritative doctrines about himself — the deposit of faith. He gives the doctrines infallibly — he states the absolute and eternal faith; he gives them authoritatively — he requires men to accept them. Men, for their part, receive him when they submit to him by believing the doctrines he requires them to believe. They submit to him, for they believe his doctrines without fully understanding them. And in believing his doctrines, they know what he tells them about himself, who he is and what he is. Thus they receive him as he presents himself through the Bible.

For Protestants, God presents himself to men by coming through the Bible to meet men directly and personally as the loving and authoritative God of history. He comes thus to meet men infallibly — he shows what he truly is. He meets men authoritatively — he is the God whose rule men should accept. Men, on their side, receive him when they know and submit to him in a personal meeting or encounter. They do not receive him through infallible and authoritative doctrines that describe him. They receive him as he comes to them directly and personally, and therefore infallibly and authoritatively.

This does not mean, in the Protestant view, that the doctrines about God in the Bible are unimportant. They are important. But their importance must be seen from their real character. They are not absolute and eternal truths that God requires men to believe about himself. Rather they are evidences that men of the Bible had a personal encounter with the loving and authoritative God of history, for they are the result of the encounter. Without it there would be no doctrines. But once the encounter takes place, doctrines develop as the language by which men try to express that encounter, how it occurred, what it means for all of life, natural and physical, and for their own lives in particular. Sometimes men borrow the language from others; sometimes they formulate it for themselves. But it is always their effort to describe the encounter.

The doctrines of the Bible, therefore, have a double importance. On the one hand, they enable those who read the Bible to know that men of the Bible had a personal encounter with the loving and authoritative God of history, and to understand something of its nature and significance. Hence, the doctrines by which men of the Bible describe their experience enable those who read the Bible to become aware of it and its meaning for them. On the other hand, the doctrines help those who have their own personal encounter with God through the Bible today to find language to express it, to put it into words. They find that the doctrines of the Bible can become the language by which they describe their encounter, how it happened, and all that it means to them.

Moreover, Protestants would emphasize, just because doctrines both inside and outside the Bible are descriptive of a personal encounter with the loving and authoritative God of history, they may vary somewhat from person to person, and from time to time. They are not the fixed doctrines of an infallible and authoritative deposit of faith. There is a general likeness about them: they refer to the same God, the loving and authoritative God of history; and men are limited in language to certain types of expression. But the doctrines vary as they describe the particular encounters God has had with different people at different times and as individual men have different ways of expressing themselves.

Protestants stress these matters because they fear greatly that doctrines can hinder men from having, through the Bible, what God wants them to have — a vital, intensely personal encounter with him. Man can hold so fervently to doctrines alone that they do not encounter God. Holding such particular doctrines, they shun an encounter with him lest their doctrines be modified; indeed, they tend to worship the doctrine and not God. Doing so, they tend to become persons who know something about God but do not know God himself. This is a misfortune from which Protestants sometimes suffer. And, Protestants believe, it is a misfortune to which Catholics are especially liable, for Catholics believe that God presents himself through doctrines absolute and final.

In any case, when Protestants say that the Bible is the infallible and authoritative Word of God, they testify to their direct and immediate encounter with God himself through the Bible. For them, the Bible is not just an ancient word from a dead past; nor is it just a book of doctrines, history, poetry, and the like. Protestants say that for them the Bible is a living Word because through it they meet the loving God who orders the events of time — the past, the present, and the future. He is the loving God who orders all natural history — who created the earth and all therein, who continues to uphold it, and who will continue to uphold it until he chooses to bring it to an end. He is the loving God who orders all human history — who has lived with men in the past, working out his purposes in their lives and speaking to them of his will; who so lives with men in the present, who will so live with men in the future, and who continues to live within the life beyond this life.

Protestants testify, that is, that through the Bible they meet the God of the Bible. He is the God who created the heavens and the earth, and upholds them with his arm. He is the God who from the beginning promised never to abandon men to their sin. He is the God who undertook to show himself in a special way through the life of a particular people, the ancient Hebrews. He is the God who saved them from bondage, who taught them of himself through their experiences as a nation, who spoke to them through the law and the prophets. He is the God who came into the world through Jesus Christ. He is the God who continues to be with the followers of Jesus Christ, giving them the joy of his fellowship and eternal life with him, making them to be his family — his people — and through them continuing to speak to the world. He is the God who at the end of the history of this time will create a new heaven and a new earth — in which men shall dwell with him and know no pain.

Protestants testify, therefore, that they go to the Bible to meet God himself. They do not go to the Bible to stop with doctrines about God — to know God by definition. They go to the Bible to meet God himself through the doctrines of the Bible, and through everything else in the Bible, through its history, its laws, its prophets, its wisdom, its letters, and the like. Thus meeting God, they find the Bible to be infallible and authoritative in the sense that there they meet him, they know him and take him as he is, as the loving and authoritative God of history.

II

Secondly, how do Protestants know that the Bible is the infallible and authoritative Word of God?

How, that is, do Protestants know that they have a personal encounter with the God of history? Protestants answer: they know it within their experience. They know they have a personal encounter with God just because they encounter him. Their experience is its own proof. They do not establish the reality or truth of the encounter by examining it from afar to see if it is real, or because someone else tells them that it is real. They know they have a personal encounter with God just as anyone knows that he has a personal encounter with another person. He knows it simply by having it. And Protestants know that they have a personal encounter with God simply by having it.

More than that, however, Protestants know that this personal encounter is not of themselves; it is of God. It is not simply that God comes to meet them through the Bible. It is also that, at the same time, God works within them through his Holy Spirit to enable them, on their side, to encounter him as he is, as the loving and authoritative God of history. For thus to encounter him they must recognize him and accept him as he is, and this the Holy Spirit enables them to do. In other words, Protestants know of their personal encounter with God through the Bible by a miracle wrought by the Holy Spirit. It is a personal miracle, one wrought in them by the Holy Spirit.

This is not to say that one Protestant who experiences the miracle gains no confidence from the similar experiences of others. When others also testify to the same experience, his confidence in the reality of his own experience increases. His is not an isolated case. And as he talks over his experience with the others, his confidence in its reality is strengthened.

But this is the crucial point: even if his were the only such experience in the world, he would still believe it. He would still believe that through the Bible he meets God personally. Others might laugh at him, call him a fool, find all kinds of ways of explaining through psychology, sociology, or economics, that he was deluded. They might even torture him, and finally threaten to put him to death as a menace to society. But he would still uphold the reality of his experience. He would still testify that as for him he knew that he had met the loving and authoritative God of history. And, God giving him strength, he would testify unto death.

But when Protestants testify that it is a miracle that they encounter God through the Bible, this is not all they can say to describe what happens. In calling the experience a personal miracle, they give it an over-all explanation: the experience is God's doing, not theirs. Still, they can analyze the experience into its elements or steps. And, as they do so, they can see how the Holy Spirit works with them at each step to bring the entire experience to pass. These steps are two:

1. Protestants believe that God speaks through the Bible as the loving and authoritative God of history.

God speaks through the records of the Bible. Some of these records incorporate scientific and historical imperfections; they have sometimes been put together in ways that make them hard to follow; they have not been transmitted from generation to generation with complete accuracy, and often they represent different levels of spiritual and moral understanding. Yet God speaks through them; and he speaks plainly enough for his essential message to be understood by all. He declares that he is the loving and authoritative God of history. He says this in the Bible's statement of his work in nature and history, in laws of religion, in accounts of special acts accomplished by him in the lives of individuals and of nations — especially the Hebrew nation — in prophetic interpretations of events from the beginning to the end of time, in books of poetry and wisdom, in letters written to churches, and especially in the story of Jesus Christ.

God speaks most fully through the Biblical record of his work in Jesus Christ. Through Jesus Christ, God most completely shows himself to be what he is, and in so doing enables men to understand better what he says in the Old Testament. For through Jesus Christ he came to act in love and authority within men's history. The Bible, in the New Testament, describes his coming through theological ideas or doctrines. It says that Jesus was the Messiah sent by God to act for him, or the Son of God who was like him, or the One in whom God dwelt. Most Protestants prefer the last description. To them it best expresses the fact that God came to earth through Jesus; and so, like Catholics, they speak of the incarnation of Christ. God came to earth in the flesh of Jesus Christ, very God in very man. Incarnate in Jesus Christ, God shows himself to be the loving and authoritative God of history. He showed it through what Christ taught; he showed it through the mastery of Christ over disease, evil forces, and evil men. He showed it through the crucifixion and resurrection of Christ. Thus God showed himself to be the God of history who, in mastery of history, acted in love to do what had to be done to secure authority over men. This is the story of salvation that a later chapter of the book describes.

Protestants believe that God speaks through the Bible. But they believe only because the Holy Spirit moves them to believe. For, without the Holy Spirit moving them, to believe would be fantastic. How can they believe that God speaks through an ancient book, and an ancient book marked with many imperfections? And how can they believe God is the loving and authoritative God of history when this is contradicted by so much that they see in the world — evil, chaos, apparent chance, death — things which suggest that there is no God of history, or if there is, that either he is not loving or he is not authoritative because he is not fully in control of history? It is incredible to believe this. Yet they do believe! They believe because the Holy Spirit moves them to believe.

2. Protestants trust the God of whom the Bible teaches. They believe in him: he *is*. They then trust him to be for them what he is, that is, the loving and authoritative God of history. When men trust another man, they surrender themselves to the direction and care of the other man. This is what Protestants do when they trust God, only they do so completely. They surrender themselves completely to

the direction and care of the God of history. They abandon their own history, life under their own control, and accept God's history, life under God's control. They allow God who orders history to order their history. They accept him as the loving authority of their lives.

How can this be? How can Protestants do this? Ordinarily they would hold on to their own history, stubbornly and grimly maintaining control over their own lives. But they give up their control. They trust God. They put God in control. This too is fantastic, incredible: it runs counter to what is natural for them to do. Once more the only explanation is the Holy Spirit. The Holy Spirit moves within them to enable them to trust God.

By the faith that is in them as both belief and trust in the God of the Bible, Protestants know that they infallibly and authoritatively encounter God through the Bible. It is the gift of God through the Holy Spirit who enables them to believe and trust the God of the Bible. Not that they have nothing to do with the coming of faith. They can reject it by refusing to believe and trust. But once they accept it, God works the miracle by which they know that through the Bible they encounter God. They need no other person or church to assure them of the encounter. They are sure of it because God himself makes them sure. Deep within them he gives them a personal assurance that as he who meets them through the Bible he is indeed the God of history.

This Protestant explanation of how men know the Bible to be the infallible and authoritative Word of God contrasts greatly with the Catholic explanation. The Catholic explanation also says that by a miracle of faith Catholics know the Bible to be the infallible and authoritative Word of God. But the Catholic explanation starts with a different conception of the Word of God; it continues on by reason apart from the help of the Holy Spirit; and finally it ends with a miracle of faith not directed immediately toward the God of the Bible, but directed toward the Bible through the infallible magisterium of the Catholic Church, that is, the absolutely true and authoritative teaching authority of the Catholic Church. The final result is that Catholics know the Bible to be the infallible and authoritative Word of God, not because they themselves know that this is so, but because they accept the declaration of the Catholic Church that it is so. To help Catholics compare their view with the Protestant view, the Catholic view will now be sketched.

For Catholics, as it has been pointed out, the Bible is the infallible Word of God in this sense: through the Bible, God reveals infallible and authoritative doctrines. It follows that men are required to believe them as being true. But here, Catholics say, they encounter a difficulty. The Bible is not altogether clear in what it says. Its language and references are sometimes confusing, its doctrines are often difficult to grasp, and every once in a while it seems to contradict itself. Obviously, Catholics continue, men cannot be completely assured that the Bible is the infallible and authoritative Word of God simply by studying the Bible. They can be completely assured only if God provides some infallible and authoritative source outside of the Bible that informs them, unmistakably and finally, that the Bible is the Word of God.

There is such a source, and Catholics find it through reason that gives way to faith. Their reason, their ability to see facts and to draw conclusions, is competent to take them far in their search without help from the Holy Spirit. So they apply their reason to the situation, and the search moves forward. The wonders of the Bible, such as its miracles, its prophecies, the holiness of its teachings, certainly make the Bible seem to be a revelation from God. But the obscurities of the Bible keep men from being sure. Certainly, however, if God intends the Bible to be a revelation, he provides a means by which he definitely shows it to be true, that is, an infallible and authoritative teacher of the Bible. It is clear, moreover, that such a teacher can be identified if the teacher's instructions have certain characteristics: oneness — they always agree with themselves; holiness — they lead to holy, or godly lives; catholicity — they are everywhere received by reasonable men; apostolicity — they agree with the teachings of the apostles, the earliest interpreters of the Bible. And the teachings of what teacher exhibit these characteristics? The teachings of the Roman Catholic Church. The Roman Catholic Church, therefore, must be the divinely appointed infallible and authoritative teacher by which men can gain assurances about the nature of the Bible. And what does the Roman Catholic Church say about the Bible? It says that the Bible is the infallible and authoritative Word of God.

But reason does not thus bring complete assurance about the nature of the Word of God; complete assurance comes only with the faith that is the gift of God. Reason always has some doubts. It can never be absolutely sure here as it can never be absolutely sure anywhere. Reason makes mistakes, and it does not necessarily possess all the facts. But through the search just described reason reduces doubts to a minimum, and by reducing doubts to a minimum, it brings men to the threshold of faith. They are now ready to go through the door of faith into the absolute assurance of the faith God gives. And, if they are willing, God gives it. God gives it as he helps them to perform a final act of faith. By this act of faith they accept, without reservations of any sort, the Roman Catholic Church as the infallible and authoritative teacher appointed by God. By this act of faith, they believe and accept what the Roman Catholic Church declares about the Bible. And when the church declares that the Bible is the infallible and authoritative Word of God they are completely and finally assured that this is what the Bible is.

Protestants are bound to admire the care and skill with which Catholics explain how they know the Bible to be the Word of God. But Protestants find some problems in the Catholic explanation — at least they are problems for Protestants. To begin with, it seems to them that Catholics start with an improper understanding of the nature of the Bible. For Protestants, God presents himself through the Bible, not in doctrines. Also, it seems to them, reason does not show the teachings of the Catholic Church to be one, holy, catholic, and apostolic as Catholics hold them to be.

Moreover, Protestants wonder if anything can be declared true by fiat, by some authoritative decision. Certainly God can declare something by fiat. He has the absolute knowledge and authority to do so. But can men? Does any man, or any group of men, have such knowledge and authority? Protestants find nothing in the Bible to suggest that they do. Besides, it is the common experience of mankind that whenever men declare a particular judgment to be absolutely true some new fact or situation always comes along to embarrass them by suggesting that their judgment was not absolutely true. Then, to hold on to their judgment without seeming to be irrational or foolish, both to themselves and to others, they have to interpret the meaning of the judgment in some fashion to agree with the new fact or situation. And in doing so again and again they really give up the judgment without admitting it, or at least it seems so to the others.

For example, Protestants wonder whether the Catholic Church may not be doing something like that with respect to what it has long held to be its official Latin translation of the Bible, the Vulgate. The Vulgate is a Latin translation of the original Hebrew and Greek Bible made largely around A.D. 400 by the great Biblical scholar, Jerome. Since the Council of Trent, convened around the middle of the sixteenth century, the Catholic Church has infallibly and authoritatively held the Vulgate to be as accurate in matters of faith and morals as the original Bible. Consequently, Catholic English translations of the Bible were made from the Vulgate. But only a few years ago, in 1943, an encyclical of Pope Pius XII encouraged Catholic scholars to translate the Bible of the original languages, in order to develop translations more accurate in details. As a result, American Catholic scholars are now engaged in translating and publishing a new English version of the Bible based on its original languages, the translation of the Confraternity of Christian Doctrine. And one of the most eminent of American Catholic scholars has written that there may be no further English translations of the Bible based on the Vulgate. To Protestants, these developments would seem to be a bypassing of the Vulgate, through which the Catholic Church is moving to a quiet recognition that the Vulgate must bow to the original Bible in all respects.

Moreover, it seems to Protestants, to explain the infallibility and authority of the Bible through an infallible and authoritative teacher presents still another difficulty: it puts a barrier between men and the God of history who would meet men through the Bible. Men tend to focus their attention upon the teacher rather than upon the Bible. His voice tends to become the Word of God rather than the Bible. His peculiar religious experience tends to become the standard of Christian experience rather than the varied religious experiences through which God speaks in the Bible. Consequently, Protestants believe, to meet the God of history most effectively and surely, men must meet him solely through the infallibility and authority of the Bible itself. They must, that is, go directly to the Bible to encounter him.

Nevertheless, of this Protestants are sure: Catholics experience the miracle of the Bible because, despite an explanation of the Bible that tends to come between them and the Bible, they do go to the Bible. They go to the Bible whenever they hear the Bible read in their services; whenever its message is brought to them in music, poetry, pictures, and symbols; whenever they read it for themselves; whenever they talk about it with others. And as they go to the Bible, the miracle of the Bible occurs. Belief and trust are born; faith is theirs as the gift of God. They encounter the God of the Bible and take him to be the loving and authoritative God of their history. And Protestants, who have the same encounter with God, know Catholics to be one with them in the common history of those who live with God.

III

Thirdly, the Bible is the only infallible and authoritative Word of God.

In saying that the Bible is the only infallible and authoritative Word of God, Protestants set aside two sources which Catholics include within the Word of God—apostolic tradition and the deuterocanonical books of the Catholic Bible. The Protestant attitude toward these sources is now given as each source is considered in turn:

1. Apostolic tradition, which for Catholics is the unwritten Word of God while the Bible is the written Word of God.

In the Catholic view, apostolic tradition is the Word of God given by Christ and the Holy Spirit to the twelve apostles or disciples of Jesus that they retained simply in their memory. They communicated it orally to their successors, the early bishops of the Catholic Church, and it was soon recorded in the ancient writings of the Catholic bishops and scholars. Since then the Catholic Church has derived its conceptions of Christianity both from the Bible and from the apostolic tradition as comprising together the Word of God.

Protestants, however, do not put apostolic tradition

within the Word of God. They experience no miracle of faith with apostolic tradition. As they contemplate the doctrine, the Holy Spirit does not move within them, bringing within them the faith by which they know of a personal encounter with God. They believe that the peculiar doctrines of apostolic tradition make it difficult for them to meet God personally as the loving and authoritative God of history. There are four doctrines which they would cite.

One: there is the idea in apostolic tradition that the Bible is the Word of God in the sense that it is an inerrant revelation of infallible and authoritative doctrine. This is not taught in the Bible itself. How this makes the personal encounter with God difficult for Protestants has already been discussed.

Two: there is the idea in apostolic tradition that the bishops of the church are infallible and authoritative teachers of the Bible. This idea of course, is what the Catholic Church would pronounce through its infallible magisterium — an idea tending, as Protestants see it, to make the personal encounter with God difficult in the same way.

Three: there is the idea in apostolic tradition that, in being saved, men receive sanctifying grace from God through the sacraments. Through sanctifying grace brought by the sacraments, God infuses into men supernatural life which makes them fit to live with him in heaven. But this idea, Protestants think, makes it difficult for men to have a personal encounter with God in which he speaks to them. When men would encounter him through sanctifying grace imparted through the sacraments, they have only an impersonal, indeed, a sort of mechanical experience of God. More will be said about this matter in the next section of the chapter and in later chapters.

Four: there is the idea in apostolic tradition that men

can do works of merit and satisfaction. Works of merit are works by which men, under God's gracious provision, increase the sanctifying grace that comes through the sacraments. Works of satisfaction are works by which men reduce the temporal penalties of their sins, the sins for which they must be punished before they can enter heaven. More will be said later about the Protestant view of such works. In general, however, Protestants think that works of satisfaction tend to come between men and a personal encounter with God. Men tend to concentrate upon them and not upon God, and they tend to make men consider God not as a God who loves because he freely gives, but as a God who attaches payment to what he brings.

2. Now we must consider the writings which for Catholics are books and parts of books included with the Bible but which are not contained in most Bibles. The problem here concerns the canon. What writings should the Christian churches officially include in the Bible?

Catholics place their additional writings with the Old Testament. These materials include a few chapters of Esther and Daniel, and seven books dealing with the period immediately before Christ: Tobias or Tobit, Judith, Wisdom, Ecclesiasticus, Baruch, and I and II Maccabees. Before the time of Christ all these writings were included in the Septuagint, a Greek version of the Old Testament used by Greek-speaking Jews living outside of Palestine, chiefly in Egypt. The Palestinian Jews rejected them. Early Christian scholars accepted the Palestinian Old Testament from the beginning. Then they began to put with it the additional writings found in the Septuagint. Since these writings were thus second in being included in the Old Testament, they are now called "deuterocanonical" — the Greek *deutero*, meaning "second," plus canon. Shortly before A.D. 400 they were approved by church councils. Finally, the Council of Trent, in the sixteenth century, declared that for the Catholic Church the Biblical Word of God includes the longer Old Testament and the present New Testament.

Protestants commonly call the deuterocanonical writings the "Old Testament Apocrypha," by which they mean, broadly speaking, that they do not regard them as belonging to the canon, the standard list of writings looked upon as the Word of God. Protestants do, however, regard the books of the Apocrypha as spiritually valuable for reading. Consequently they translate them for reading, and sometimes they bind them between the Old and New Testaments.

For Catholics to understand why Protestants do not consider their deuterocanonical materials as canonical, it is necessary for them to understand the general Protestant position on the statement of a canon by a church. This general Protestant position can be seen through two observations:

For one thing, Protestants believe that a church can properly make a given list of writings canonical, provided it does so to identify the sources of its own personal encounter, that is, its members' personal encounter, with God. A church is made up of people who experience a personal encounter with God through certain writings. As a church these people can properly list those writings as canonical, provided they do so for two reasons. They do so properly if they make the writings canonical and standard for their own use; and if they do so to suggest to others that through these writings the others too can share their experience of God. It was in this way, Protestants believe, that the early church developed a canon. Moreover, they believe, it was in this way that the churches of the Protestant Reformation decided to continue the canon of the early church, but without the deuterocanonical materials. Certainly no church, they are convinced, can fix a canon through an infallible magisterium. A church cannot be authoritative over the writings through which God speaks lest it attempt to be authoritative over God.

For the second thing, Protestants believe that a church should never finally close a canon, but should always be ready to reconsider and restate its canon. If it finally closes its canon, it may shut itself off from writings through which God would speak to it. No church has an infallible magisterium thus to refuse to hear what God would speak, and if it does so without claiming to have an infallible magisterium, it acts as though it had one. Consequently, with the passage of time, churches should always be ready to reexamine their canons, perhaps to substract, perhaps to add.

In the light of this general Protestant attitude toward the canon, the Protestant position on the Catholic deuterocanonical writings of the Old Testament can be quickly stated. These writings Protestants now omit from their canon, that is, from their Bible, for this reason: they do not believe that through them God speaks to men personally as he does through the other books in their canon. They do not believe that they are so taught of the Holy Spirit. On the other hand, it is entirely possible that sometimes Protestants may believe themselves to be taught otherwise by the Holy Spirit. In that case they would reopen their canon and include one or more of the deuterocanonical books. In fact, some Protestants are wondering whether that time has not already come.

IV

Fourthly, the Bible is its own one and infallible and authoritative teacher.

In saying that the Bible is its own one and infallible and authoritative teacher, Protestants mean this: they must constantly return directly to the Bible to learn what God has to teach them about his history and theirs. There they must meet him regularly to know more freely the meaning of his past, present, and future action. There they must meet him regularly to know more fully his will for them. And they must do so directly, just as they first met him directly. For their encounter with God continues to be a personal encounter. Men have, then, no other and infallible teacher than the Bible through which they continue to be taught by God.

This does not mean that men should return to the Bible apart from the experiences of their lives. The God who continually teaches them through the Bible is the God of history. Through those events of history he puts new questions to men, faces them with fresh responsibilities to be understood and accepted, shatters their old and inadequate views about his will, calls them to re-examine the truth about his will which they have forgotten or set aside. And all this he does to send them to the Bible to discover the answers he has for them.

Men must, Protestants stress, go directly to the Bible to be taught of God. Their encounter with God is to continue to be a personal encounter through the Bible. Besides, God may have something to say to them individually, or to particular groups of them. And also, no single person or group of persons can state either infallibly and authoritatively or simply authoritatively what God teaches. The divine teacher is always right, but his students, with human limitations and sins, always score much below a hundred. There are no " A " students in God's school! Of course, the ideas of other students should be heeded. God's students need to share their knowledge of God so that all can come to fuller knowledge. But, Protestants believe, no individual, group, or church can speak for God.

It is clear, of course, that Protestants cannot accept the continuing infallible magisterium of the Roman Catholic Church, the power the church claims from God to teach infallibly and authoritatively what God says in the Bible. This is the power the Catholic Church has used through the centuries to decide doctrinal points on which Catholics were previously allowed to disagree among themselves.

For example, at the Council of Trent, about 1560, it fixed the number of the sacraments at seven. And since 1850, it has required all Catholics to believe in the Immaculate Conception of Mary — her birth without sin (1854); the infallibility of the pope in matters of faith and morals (1870); and the Assumption of the Virgin Mary — her bodily ascent into heaven (1950). Those who do not accept its doctrinal decisions the Catholic Church excommunicates, which means they cannot be saved while they remain excommunicated.

Incidentally, Protestants accept none of these recent doctrines. Protestants respect what Catholic popes have to say, but only as one fallible teacher among many other fallible teachers. And Protestants have great esteem for the Virgin Mary — after all she was the mother of Jesus. But Protestants think that Jesus himself warned against the exaltation of his mother above other persons when he said, "My mother and my brothers are those who hear the word of God and do it" (Luke 8:21). Protestants fear that Catholic emphasis upon the importance of Mary tends to obscure the meaning of the incarnation. For God came to the earth to meet men, not in Mary, but in Jesus Christ.

It is clear, also, that Protestants cannot accept the authority of the Roman Church when it teaches authoritatively, but not infallibly. There are, for example, the decisions of the Catholic Biblical Commission, which was founded in 1902. This Commission furthers the study of the Bible along Catholic lines, and Protestants are indebted to it as well as Catholics. The decisions of the Commission, when approved by the pope, are not infallible — they may be changed; but once announced they must be sincerely received by Catholics. If a Catholic scholar questions the reasons given for them, he may inform the Commission privately of his views and the Commission may change its mind. But he cannot question the Commission's decision publicly; that would be to show disrespect and disobedience for proper authority. Protestants, on the other hand, never believe merely because anyone tells them to believe; and if they want to disagree, they can shout it to the housetops — and they often do!

For Protestants, the Bible is an open book, open for all Protestants to study for themselves independently of the teaching authority of any church. It is true, Protestants acknowledge, that in some places the Bible is too difficult for the average person to understand: he needs expert help — which is why Protestants welcome the help of both Protestant and Catholic scholars. But Protestants believe that on the whole the Bible is plain enough so that the average person can truly confront God through it without expert guidance. Catholics, on the other hand, believe that the Bible is so difficult that no one can be allowed to study it except under the guidance of the Catholic Church. This means, among other things, that Catholics can study only those versions of the Bible approved by the Catholic Church — Protestants, however, are free from churchly controls. They can study any version they choose, and seek out the God of the Bible in any way they choose. They can even make and publish their own translations of the Bible.

But this Protestants would emphasize: they do not exercise their freedom in order to avoid authority — in order simply to be free; they exercise their freedom in order to be subject to authority — the sole authority of God as they meet him in the Bible. Protestants claim no right to the absolute freedom which derides all authority; in making such a claim they would be denying God's authority. They must, they believe, submit to God's authority. But that they cannot do if they submit to what others say about the Bible. They can submit to God's authority only if they have freedom to meet him for themselves through the Bible — to study the Bible for themselves. They must be free from other authorities in order to bow before the authority of God. Hence Protestants study the

Bible, not to show themselves free before God, but to show themselves submissive to God.

It follows that Protestants are free to read any books bearing in any way upon the Bible that they may wish to read. There is no Protestant Index. The Catholic Church, exercising its infallible magisterium, protects its people from wrong beliefs through its Prohibitory Index, a list of books not to be read by Catholics, and through its Expurgatory Index, a list of books from which certain passages are to be removed before Catholics read them. But Protestants are free to read all books, whatever they may say about the Bible directly, or however they may oppose the Bible indirectly. Certainly, some books may threaten their faith in the God of the Bible, and their fellow Protestants and Protestant churches should counsel them about such books. But Protestants are subject only to God; and if they are to avoid any particular books, they must do so only because they themselves believe that to be God's will for them.

Finally, Protestants would assure Catholics of this: as they study the Bible, they welcome the opportunity to study the Bible with Catholics. This is a part of their freedom before men and submission to God. They would study the Bible with Catholics to learn what God is teaching Catholics through the Bible. Catholics have much to teach them, Protestants are sure. Hence, Protestants would join them in a fuller meeting with the loving and authoritative God of history who encounters both Catholics and Protestants through the Bible.

CHAPTER IV *The Church*

If Protestants are people of the Bible, Catholics are people of the church. Whereas Protestants have faith that they encounter God directly in the Bible, Catholics have faith in their church's assurance that through the Bible God reveals the deposit of faith. Protestants through faith look to the Bible directly for assurance that they encounter God; Catholics through faith look first to the infallible magisterium of the Roman Catholic Church. Consequently, whereas Protestants base their Christian experience directly upon the God of the Bible, Catholics base their Christian experience upon what the Catholic Church informs them about the God of the Bible. Catholics, therefore, are people of the church, and more particularly, of the Roman Catholic Church.

Since Catholics are people of the church, it is fitting for Protestants to go on immediately to explain the Protestant view of the church. But beyond that, Protestants are happy on their own account to describe their view of the church. For the church is dear to Protestants as well as to Catholics. One evidence is the fact that so many of their best-loved hymns are about the church and its blessed place in their lives. Here, for example, is a stanza of such a hymn:

> "I love thy church, O God!
> Her walls before thee stand,
> Dear as the apple of thine eye,
> And graven on thy hand."

The church *is* important to Protestants, so important that they cannot think of Christianity without it. Indeed, they cannot experience Christianity without it. For Protestants, the church belongs to Christianity just as surely as does the Bible.

The Protestant view of the church is now described in connection with four principal Protestant convictions about the church. The first of these beliefs is fundamental to the others, the others deriving in one way or another from it.

I

First, Protestants believe that Jesus Christ alone is head of the church.

The book of The Acts relates how the church began. Jesus ascended into heaven. But those who followed him upon the earth — his disciples and other followers — knew that through him they had become a new kind of community in the world. Through him they met the loving and authoritative God of history, and thus they became the special people of that God. They were saved, as will be described in the next chapter, to sonship with God. And they began to live together as the family of God, worshiping together and helping each other. Then they did something more. They began to tell others about God's work in Christ. As they did so, "the Lord added to their number day by day those who were being saved" (Acts 2:47). Thus others had the experiences of the first disciples, the experience of meeting God in Christ and becoming sons of God. Moreover, continues the book of The Acts, the disciples and others, especially Paul, went into many lands telling about God's work in Christ. And as they told of that work, there were still others who had their experience. They accepted the loving authority of God in Christ, were saved, and became members of the family of God, or the new community now being called the church, the household of God. And so the church came into being.

In the Protestant view, the New Testament makes very clear that the only leader of the new community of God, the church, is Jesus Christ. In the letters to the Ephesians and the Colossians this is put into a figure of speech. The new community is thought of as the continuing body of Christ in the world, because through it he continues to speak and act. And Christ is called the head of that body which is the church. Says the letter to the Ephesians, "The God of our Lord Jesus Christ . . . has put all things under his feet and made him the head over all things for the church, which is his body." (Eph. 1:17, 22-23.)

In the Gospels there is another New Testament passage understood by Protestants to refer to the leadership or headship of Christ over the church. In Matt., ch. 16, Christ asks Peter, "Who do you say that I am?" Peter answers, "You are the Christ, the Son of the living God." And Jesus responds, "You are Peter, and on this rock I will build my church." The rock here may be the rock of Peter's confession, "You are the Christ, the Son of the living God," which is the way the passage was generally interpreted by the scholars of the early church. Or the rock may be Peter as a representative of all those who enter the church because they share his belief: the church will be made up of men like Peter who know that they have met God through Jesus Christ. In either case, the church exists through Jesus Christ, which is another way of saying that Christ is the head of the church.

Catholics will understand that reference is made to the Protestant understanding of the passage from Matthew partly because the Catholic Church, through its infallible magisterium, interprets it differently. For the Catholic Church the rock is Peter himself as the head of the church. Christ, says the Catholic Church, was appointing Peter to be the first pope, or head of the church. Then the Catholic Church goes on to conclude from other New Testament passages, from apostolic tradition, and from history, that Christ also appointed Peter's successors to be the continuing popes or heads of the church.

Protestants, however, cannot agree. Protestants have great respect for the popes of the Catholic Church in general. The qualification " in general " is made because Protestants have no more respect for the lives some of the popes have lived than do Catholics! But Protestants do respect the popes for their continuing witness in so many ways to the God of the Bible, and for the splendid lives that so many of them have lived. Christendom would be the poorer without them. Nevertheless, Protestants find no basis inside or outside the Bible for recognizing them to be heads of the church appointed by Christ. In their conviction, Christ himself and alone is the head of the church.

Accepting Christ alone as head of the church, Protestants allow no one in their churches the absolute and final authority exercised by the pope of the Catholic Church. In the Catholic Church the pope is a spiritual king with autocratic powers. He can command without consulting anyone, and no one can appeal from his judgments. In all Protestant churches no individual or group of individuals has such powers. All persons exercise whatever powers they possess subject to the higher authority of Jesus Christ, and anyone can appeal from their judgments to Jesus Christ. Accordingly, while the Catholic Church is an absolute spiritual monarchy, the Protestant churches are spiritual democracies. Protestant churches, acknowledging only Christ as their head, do not concentrate complete authority in one individual or group, but distribute authority among all their people.

Moreover, because Protestants acknowledge Christ alone to be head of the church, authority exercised by and within their churches is declarative only. That is, no Protestant church and no Protestant church official or official group can issue commands so binding upon Protestants that

Protestants sin in disobeying them. Protestants sin only when they disobey the head of the church, Jesus Christ. No human being or group of human beings can legislate for Jesus Christ. They can only declare what seems to them to accord with the will of Jesus Christ. When they presume to legislate for Jesus Christ, they attempt to take Christ's place as head of the church; and that is sin. The Protestant position is that God alone, through Jesus Christ, is Lord of men's consciences—which is to say that God alone determines for men what is right and what is wrong.

For this reason Protestant churches have no laws similar to the Catholic Church's "precepts of the church." The Catholic Church believes that it has power from Christ to use its own judgment in formulating religious laws about specific matters not covered by the Bible, and to declare disobedience to those laws to be sin. Protestants allow their churches to make no such laws. No church, they believe, Protestant or Catholic, has power from Christ to specify anything to be sin. Only Christ himself, the head of the church, has that power. A church can suggest what to it seems wise or unwise, proper or improper, but it can do no more. It can only state its opinion. And it must base that opinion, not on its own judgment, but on the Word of God found in the Bible. There God himself says what sin is. When men on the other hand, use their own judgments to say what sin is, they try to be what no man dare try to be: they try to be God.

Similarly, Protestants recognize no one or no group within their churches as having power to forgive sins. Catholics, of course, believe their priests to have such power from Christ. But Protestants nowhere discover in the Bible that Christ gives the church as a group, or the church represented by its clergy, the power to forgive sins. The church, through its teaching of God's Word in the Bible, can only help men to know what sin is and to realize that God forgives sin. It is in this sense that Matt. 16:19 is to be understood. There Christ says that he gives Peter

" the keys of the kingdom of heaven " so that what Peter binds or looses on earth is also bound or loosed in heaven. Christ, however, is not conferring upon Peter authority to forgive sins, and through Peter as head of the church conferring authority to forgive sins upon the church and its clergy. Instead, Christ is referring to the authority he gives the church, founded upon himself, to set forth the message of sin and redemption expressed in him and through him in the Bible. The actual forgiveness of sins is reserved to God. Only God can forgive sins. Once more, men dare not try to be God!

II

Secondly, Protestants believe that the church is composed of those who submit to Jesus Christ as head of the church.

Since Christ is head of the church, all those who submit to Christ constitute the church. This is the position expressed by Paul in I Cor. 12:12-13: " For just as the body is one and has many members, and all the members of the body, though many, are one body, so it is with Christ. For by one Spirit we were all baptized into one body." The church is Christ's body; and individuals become parts of that body as they accept the directions of its head, who is Christ alone. In this view Protestants differ from Catholics. Catholics become members of the church by submitting to the pope. Protestants become members of the church by submitting to Jesus Christ.

Moreover, Protestants believe, by thus becoming members of the church they become members of the catholic or universal church. For Catholics the catholic or universal church is their Church; and so they call it the Catholic Church. In their judgment it is catholic or universal because throughout the world there are those who submit to the pope and in that submission constitute the church. But for Protestants the catholic or universal church of which they speak is catholic or universal because everywhere throughout the world there are those who submit to Jesus Christ and in that submission constitute the church. To this catholic church, declare Protestants, they belong, and, they quickly add, so do Roman Catholics who submit to Jesus Christ.

For, according to this Protestant view, one is not a member of the catholic church because one belongs to a particular organization, such as the Methodist, Baptist, Presbyterian, and Episcopalian Churches, or the Roman Catholic Church. One is a member of the catholic church because one submits to Christ. The catholic church is not a particular organization. It is the vast fellowship of those everywhere made to be a fellowship through their common submission to Jesus Christ.

Similarly, all particular organized churches, through the submission of their people to Jesus Christ, are parts of that catholic church. Consequently they can all be called catholic churches. For Protestants, it would be proper to speak not only of the Roman Catholic Church; it would be proper to speak also of the Methodist Catholic Church, the Baptist Catholic Church, the Lutheran Catholic Church, the Presbyterian Catholic Church and the like. For Protestants, all these particular organized churches, including the Roman Catholic Church, are denominations, that is, divisions of the single catholic church.

What is more, for Protestants, therefore, their denominations are not new churches; they are old churches, as old as the catholic church properly conceived, which is as old as Christianity. To be sure, Protestant denominations are new in this sense: they have been organized since the time of the Protestant Reformation, about four hundred years ago. But in a deeper sense they are old as new forms of life are old. New forms of life are old since they are expressions of life that has continued from the beginning. And Protestant denominations are old since they are expressions of what has continued from the beginning of Christianity, the catholic church composed of those who submit to Christ. So, fundamentally, it is incorrect to say that Protestant churches have broken away from the catholic church and are therefore new. Rather, it is correct to say that they have become further divisions within the catholic church and are therefore old.

This catholic church of which Protestants speak is, for them, the true church. If the true church must be, as Catholics require it to be, one, holy, catholic, and apostolic, then this church meets those requirements. It is *one:* its members are one with Jesus Christ, with each other, and with Christians of all the ages in their common submission to Jesus Christ. It is *holy:* its members, submitting to Jesus Christ, accept God's forgiveness and become manifestations of his holy life. It is *catholic:* its members are found throughout the world. It is *apostolic:* it is composed from generation to generation of those who are the spiritual descendants of the apostles, the first Christians.

No single organized church is the true church, but all organized churches are true churches by submitting to Jesus Christ. By existing within the true and catholic church, they are true churches just as they are catholic churches. What the whole is, they, its parts, also are. Through being parts of the true church they too are true churches. For this reason, Protestants cannot agree with Catholics that the Catholic Church, or more specifically, the Roman division of the catholic church, is the only true church. The Roman Church is just one true church in the same way that other churches are true churches: it is a true church in so far as it submits to Christ.

Furthermore, Protestants believe, organized churches must demonstrate their submission by actively seeking to do his will. To find his will they must search the Bible. And they must apply his will to every aspect of their corporate life, to their government, beliefs, worship, and moral activities. They must try to organize themselves according to his pattern, believing according to his thoughts, worshiping according to his directions, doing good according to his will. In this fashion, as organized churches, they demonstrate from day to day that it is submission to Christ as their head that makes them true churches.

But no organized church, Protestants are convinced, achieves all this perfectly: every church only imperfectly expresses the will and mind of Christ. There is no perfect church any more than there are perfect individuals. Just as individual persons are rendered imperfect by the limitations of their humanity and their sins, so churches, composed of those individual persons, are rendered imperfect. Ignorance and sin impair their obedience to Christ. In fact, organized churches are often more imperfect than the individuals who compose them; for men as a group are often more imperfect than men as individuals. So it is that churches, like other groups, suffer from mass inertia, on the one hand, or from mass hysteria, on the other hand, and consequently fall short of perfect submission to Jesus Christ. No organized church is a perfect church — in government, beliefs, worship, or morality.

Nevertheless, Protestants believe, it is to these churches as parts of the catholic church that Christ has given the task of making known to men the revelation of God given through him. Christ is their head; they are the parts of his body, and as the parts of his body they must express his mind and will. What Christ wants men to believe and to do, they must try to discover and make known. In so doing, since God's purpose through Christ is to rescue men from their sin and their ignorance, they make Christ known as Savior. What is more, they are the saving instruments of Christ. This, Protestants believe, is the case with all churches true and catholic by reason of their submission to Jesus Christ. They are all saving instruments of Christ.

III

Thirdly, Protestants believe that the church is composed entirely of priests.

Since Christ is head of the church, all Christians as members of the church are priests. A priest is one who stands between God and men, representing God to men and men to God. But in Christ, the head of the church, God stands directly before Christians with no one appointed to stand between. God who in Christ directly confronts Christians is directly confronted by them. In other words, they are their own priests. So in The First Letter of Peter (ch. 2:5) all Christians are instructed to be "a holy priesthood." And since all Christians are priests in the church, they exercise what Protestants call "the priesthood of the believer," that is, their right to represent themselves before God.

To be sure, Protestants have clergymen in their churches; but Protestants do not ascribe to them the unique priestly character that Catholics ascribe to their priests. Both Protestant clergymen and Catholic priests are ordained and through their ordination receive powers not exercised by the laity. But Protestants and Catholics differ about how ordination confers those powers. Catholics believe that ordination is a sacrament; hence the supernatural life imparted by it gives the souls of their priests a distinctively spiritual character. This distinctive spiritual character, not shared by the laity, makes them a priestly class apart from the laity. Protestants believe that ordination confers powers upon their clergymen by inducting them into an office. But it imparts no distinctive spiritual power to them. Although they have the special responsibilities of a particular office in the church, they continue to be spiritually one in character with the people. Protestant clergymen, in the Protestant view, are simply specialized priests among Christians who are also priests.

For this reason, Protestants confess their sins only to God, not to their clergymen. Since God is the source of righteousness, all men's sins are ultimately against him, and men must confess their sins to God. But, Protestants believe, men must confess their sins directly to God, not to any priestly intermediary, or go-between. When the psalmist wrote in Ps. 32:5, he spoke of a personal act that should be the act of all Christians: "I will confess my transgressions to the Lord." All Christians should confess their sins to God — directly. Unlike Catholics, therefore, Protestants do not confess their sins to priests. They confess their sins to God alone, whom they meet directly in Christ, the one head of the church.

Furthermore, since it is the Protestant view that all members of the church are priests, the lay members of Protestant churches share very largely with their clergymen in the government of the church. Of course Catholic laymen hold a variety of responsibilities in the government of the Catholic Church. But these responsibilities are given them by the priests and bishops of the Catholic Church in whom the entire authority of the church is vested. Protestant laymen, on the other hand, hold their responsibilities in the government of the Protestant Church as a *right*. Their responsibilities belong to them — neither given to them nor to be taken away by their clergymen — because they participate in the priesthood of believers.

Some illustrations drawn from general Protestant practices show how much Protestant laymen share in the government of their churches. Local Protestant churches have official boards, elected by laymen and composed of laymen, which largely direct their life. The official boards not only manage property; they also admit new church members. Also, Protestant laymen share in the ordination of their clergy. Usually they do this through their lay representatives who join with the clergy in approving candidates for ordination. In some Protestant churches, however, the laymen actually ordain their own clergy. Similarly, Protestant laymen share in the naming of their pastors. Through the votes of their representatives or through their own votes they help to determine what clergymen will become the pastors of their churches.

Protestant churches, therefore, are much more churches of the people than is the Catholic Church. In the Catholic Church the people are ministered to by the Catholic clergy. In the Protestant churches the people minister along with the Protestant clergy. Responsibilities for service in and through the Protestant churches are divided among laymen and clergymen, with the members of each group possessing by right their share. Protestant laymen and Protestant clergymen are all ministers of the things of God done in and through Christ's church; they differ only in function as the members of each group minister in the particular way assigned to them. In the Protestant churches there is but one ministry, or priesthood. That is the ministry, or the priesthood, of all the people.

To this section it may be added, as a kind of postscript, that Protestant churches further show themselves to be churches of the people by the fact that their clergy marry. Catholic priests do not marry because the Catholic Church believes that they can be more effective workmen without the responsibilities of married life. Of course the Catholic Church makes an exception in the instance of their Uniat priests, priests of certain groups that through the years have entered the Roman Church from the Greek Orthodox Church. Uniat priests may be married provided they marry before ordination. But all Protestant ministers may marry if they choose because the Protestant Church believes that they can ordinarily serve most effectively living the normal and usual life of the other members of the church. Among other things, themselves married, they can understand more fully the problems of marriage, and they can help to set an example of ideal Christian married life.

IV

Fourthly, Protestants believe that Christians have the right to seek God's will by forming their own particular church organizations.

Since Christ is head of the church, Christians have the

right to form their own particular church organizations or denominations, provided they do so for one reason: to seek Christ's will for the church. They have no right to form denominations of their own for reasons not connected with Christ's will — for frivolous, personal, worldly reasons, that is, sinful reasons. But they are bound to obey, inside the church as well as outside the church, Christ's command recorded in Matt. 6:33: "Seek first . . . [God's] kingdom and his righteousness." Here the command is to seek God's will as made known in Jesus Christ. If, in obedience to that command, Christians regard themselves obliged to form a particular church organization or denomination, then, Protestants believe, they have the right to do so. For they must possess the right in order to obey the command.

In determining Christ's will for the church in this connection, Christians may relate it to all the elements that make up particular denominations. These include denominational government, beliefs, worship, and conduct. Since Christ is head of the church, all these matters must harmonize with his will. But some persons may believe with all sincerity that in existing denominations these matters do not harmonize with his will. In that case then, Protestants believe, they have the right to form other denominations organized according to what they believe to be Christ's will. They have the right to form denominations with governments, beliefs, worship, and conduct agreeable with what they believe to be the will of Christ.

This right, Protestants recognize, must be exercised with caution. No person can expect others to agree with him in every respect, and some differences between individuals are minor. Besides, exercise of the right to organize another denomination, however legitimate, like all things human, has its unfortunate consequences. The adding of another denomination to those already existing furthers a degree of confusion and competition among denominations; this obscures their unity in their common head, Jesus Christ, and diminishes the effectiveness of their service for him. No group of Christians, therefore, should exercise the right to form another denomination unless they are thoroughly persuaded that in no other way can they secure the government, beliefs, worship, or conduct that they are convinced represent Christ's will for the church.

When, however, they are thus persuaded, they are responsible before Christ to act accordingly. Christ alone is head of the church; they owe their loyalty to him alone; and if they can fully express their loyalty to him only by forming a new denomination, this they must do. Responsible to him, they need not accept what other denominations believe to be his will. When the situation appears sufficiently serious to them, they must employ their right to establish denominations agreeable with what they believe to be his will. Their right to establish denominations of their own is not something they can continuously reject. There are times when their responsibility to Christ requires them to exercise their right to organize denominations of their own.

But, Protestants believe, when Christians find themselves in such times they must respect the right of others to remain in their own denominations. They must respect others' sense of responsibility to Christ which inspires them to exercise their right to remain in their own denominations. Since Christ is head of the church, one group of Christians has the right to serve Christ according to its convictions by establishing its own denomination, and other groups of Christians have the right to serve Christ by continuing with denominations already established. Under Christ the one right is equal to the other.

In harmony with these convictions Protestants have formed their different particular church organizations or denominations. Some of these denominations go back four hundred years to the days of the Protestant Reformation when many people left the Catholic Church. Other denominations have been organized since then by people who leave various Protestant denominations to form denominations of their own. Added together, the total of Protestant denominations is large — there are over two hundred in the United States. But most Protestants belong to a few large denominations. As was pointed out in the first chapter, eight denominations include 85 per cent of Protestant church worship.

Although Catholicism is organized into one particular church organization, Catholicism has within it a diversity somewhat comparable to Protestant denominationalism. (This is aside from the fact that for Protestants the Catholic Church is itself a denomination.) There are Polish Catholics, and German Catholics, and French Catholics, and American Catholics, and Italian Catholics, and the other national groups of Catholics, with their own laws of the church, with their own spirit and customs, and, it must be added, with a considerable degree of rivalry among them. There are Jesuits, and Dominicans, and Franciscans, and Benedictines and Cistercians, and other religious orders, with their own rules, with their own theological and liturgical peculiarities, and, it must be added again, with a considerable degree of rivalry among them.

Despite their denominationalism, however, Protestants have a deep sense of Christian unity with one another. This appears in practical ways. Protestants freely move from one Protestant denomination to another. Protestant laymen of one denomination worship without hesitation in the churches of other denominations, and often take their membership from one denomination to another. Protestant clergymen of different denominations lead worship services together. Indeed, Protestant clergymen commonly transfer from one denomination to another without their new denomination requiring them to be reordained. And there is the Protestant ecumenical movement. Of this more will be said in the final chapter. This much now: the Protestant ecumenical movement is an effort to achieve a greater degree of co-operation and unity among Christians of all denominations. As one result, Protestants have been increasingly successful in achieving denominational unions.

Three deepening convictions among Protestants inspire them to their sense of unity with one another. The first conviction is that the different organized churches are one church. They are one church, one catholic church, through their same loyalty to Jesus Christ. He is their one Lord who binds them all together. The second conviction is that the churches can attain greater unity relative to what they believe to be God's will in matters of church government, beliefs, worship, and conduct. Many times, for example, their differences derive from misunderstandings about words, or from events of the past now largely without meaning. The third conviction is that the denominations are separate denominations in part because of sin. The reasons given by their members to justify them are sometimes the frivolous, personal, and worldly reasons that are sinful reasons.

Still Protestants continue to uphold their right to denominations of their own, provided they deem these denominations to be necessary to their obedience of Christ. They must obey Christ in thought, worship, and life, according to what they believe to be the will of Christ. And if denominations of their own are required to enable them so to obey Christ, then, they believe, they have the right to such denominations. Some of them, despite the ecumenical movement, will organize other denominations. For in doing so, Protestants believe themselves not to be perverse or divisive, but to be simply what all Christians must be, loyal to Christ, the one head of the church.

CHAPTER V | *Salvation*

Many Catholics pray fervently for the salvation of Protestants, and Protestants are grateful. And when Catholics pray for the conversion of Protestants, Protestants understand. Catholics are prompted by the sincere belief that, though Protestants do not necessarily go to hell, they are much more likely to go to heaven by becoming Catholics. For in the Catholic view, God has committed to the Catholic Church the special knowledge and means by which he saves men most effectively.

Protestants, however, find their own experience of salvation fully adequate. It comes, they believe, with a proper interpretation of the Bible. And so, just as sincerely as Catholics, they hold their view of salvation and testify to it. Their view will be described here in connection with: first, the nature of salvation; second, what God does to save men; third, what men do to be saved; and fourth, the possibility of salvation for non-Christians.

I

First, the nature of salvation or, What does it mean for men to be saved? Protestants answer: Salvation means that men become the sons of God, with all which that involves.

Before salvation men are in deep trouble. Men refuse to be God's sons. God is their father, but they reject him. They act as though their lives were not from him, and they persist in disobeying him. They are rebels against him — sinners. As such, they suffer penalties. They lose the honor and joy of being the sons of God. They become subject to death, not simply physical death, but the death that is continuing life apart from God, that is, eternal death. Also, they experience earthly anxieties and misfortunes. Nevertheless, they have no desire to become the sons of God. And in any case, their guilt stands between them and God.

To begin with, they are saved from the rebellion by which they war against God, from the guilt through which they are unworthy to become the sons of God, and from the penalties under which they suffer for their sins. Then they are saved to sonship with God, and the blessings that come with it. They know the honor and the joys of the sons of God. They receive eternal life. Were men saved to the wonder of sonship with God only to lose it by death, they would be "of all men most to be pitied" (I Cor. 15:19). But they do not lose it by death. They are saved to eternal life, the life of sonship with God that goes on after death. Moreover, as the sons of God, they are saved to growing obedience toward God. And though they still suffer anxieties and misfortunes because of their continuing sin, their sufferings are disciplines, means of learning obedience, not penalties.

Salvation, for Protestants, does not involve purgatory. For Catholics, of course, it does. Catholics believe that men are saved from the eternal penalties of sin, the pains of hell. But they do not believe that men are saved from the temporal penalties of sin, the penalties they must endure before they can enter heaven. These penalties men must suffer either on earth or in purgatory, and only a few saints escape purgatory. Most men suffer in purgatory for a longer or shorter time. Protestants, however, find nothing in the Bible that speaks directly of purgatory; and, besides, purgatory contradicts the Biblical teaching that men are saved from all the penalties of their sin. Since men are saved from all the penalties of sin, in dying they pass immediately from earth to heaven.

This which is men's salvation is the work of God. But men must accept it from him. The next two sections describe, therefore, what God does to save men, and what men do to be saved.

II

Secondly, what does God do to save men?

This question eventually requires the division of men into Christians and non-Christians. In the historical sense, Christians are those saved in their knowledge of God's saving work in Jesus Christ. They do not include those who have never known Christ — children dying in infancy, persons who lived before Christ, and persons after Christ who never heard or hear of him. How these persons are saved, the last section of the chapter describes. This section and the next relate only to men who know of salvation through Christ.

What, then, does God do to save men who hear the Christian message? As Protestants see it, God has done something in the past: loving men, God came to the world through Jesus Christ for men's salvation; and God does something in the present: loving men, God comes to the world through the Bible for men's salvation.

In the past, even before men sinned, God decided to save men simply because he loved them. On this Protestants and Catholics agree. God decided to save men even though they did not deserve it. As his creatures, men deserve nothing from God; besides, they are sinners. Nor did God decide to save men to benefit himself. Eventually, in Christ, salvation cost him the cross. God decided to save men simply out of love, free from considerations of men's worth or his own self-interest. Salvation comes to men, therefore, as the free gift of God's love.

In deciding to save men, God faced two problems. One problem was that of atonement. Refusing to be God's sons, men are not at one with him. And they are kept from being one with him by their rebellious disposition and by their guilt. How could their rebelliousness and guilt be overcome? The other problem was that of eternal death. Refusing to be God's sons, men are subject to eternal death, life apart from God now and beyond the grave. How could God give men eternal life by which they can live on in sonship with him beyond this life?

The first step God took to solve these problems was the incarnation. God came to earth in Jesus Christ. "God was in Christ." (II Cor. 5:19.) Incarnated in Christ, God proceeded to work out men's salvation.

In Jesus Christ, God solved the problem of atonement. "God was in Christ reconciling the world to himself," that is, drawing himself and men together. God solved the problem of the atonement through Christ's death upon the cross. By Christ's death men's rebelliousness was overcome. "And you, who once were estranged and hostile in mind, doing evil deeds, he has now reconciled . . . by his death." (Col. 1:21.) And by Christ's death men's guilt was taken away. "In [Christ] we have redemption through his blood, the forgiveness of our trespasses." (Eph. 1:7.) To do these things God, through Christ, sacrificed himself: he gave himself upon the cross for men's good.

Just how God accomplished these things by the cross, Protestants find hard to understand, although they are sure he did. Like Catholics, they discover in the Bible bases for several explanations, or theories, of the atonement. Most Protestants think as follows. In Christ's death God removed the rebellion of men by showing them how much he loves them. Through the agony and death of the cross, men know the marvel of his love for them. In the face of love, rebelliousness disappears; and so, through the love of the cross, God overcomes men's rebellion. Furthermore, in Christ's death God removed the guilt of men by enduring the sufferings they owe as the penalties for their sins. Hence their guilt, with its penalties, is discharged. God did not, however, forgive men because of the cross. In a sense, God had already forgiven men, back when first he decided to save them. The cross is the means by which he took away their guilt.

Then God solved the problem of eternal death. He did it by conquering death through the cross. Through Christ's death God entered into death and overcame the negative and evil forces by which men, in their guilt, are slain. He "disarmed the principalities and powers and made a public example of them, triumphing over them in" Christ. (Col. 2:15.) The evidence of that triumph is the resurrection of Christ. Death could not hold him. And Christ's triumph is the triumph of men saved to sonship with God. Because of it God can give them eternal life. How this is possible is a mystery, but a mystery no greater than God's gift of life in the first place. But this is sure: through Christ "death is swallowed up in victory" (I Cor. 15:54, 57).

Since the resurrection of Christ was the climax of what God did in Christ, Protestants emphasize a living Christ. So it is, for example, that Protestant pictures of Christ represent him as vibrantly alive, not on a cross, or wearing a crown of thorns, or with a face pale and drawn with agony. On the other hand, it seems to Protestants that Catholics have a strong tendency to emphasize a dead Christ. Catholic pictures commonly represent a Christ in agony; the Christ of Catholic crucifixes is dead; and Christ is continuously sacrificed in Catholic Masses. Protestants know nothing of a constantly suffering Christ. Christ suffered "once for all" (Rom. 6:10). For Protestants the cross is empty. Christ was taken down from the cross, buried, and raised again. He triumphed over death. And he lives!

But there is also what God does today to save men. Loving men, God comes to them through the Bible for their salvation.

God's love never fails; so God comes today through the Bible to save men. He speaks to men through the Bible, making known to them what he has done to save them. Thus he acts now to save them. Whether he can save them depends upon their responses. But in his love he comes to save them.

Coming to men through the Bible, God calls them from their rebelliousness. He does not answer their rebellion with wrath. That would only make them more rebellious. He answers their rebellion with love. He points them to his love exhibited upon the cross, a love older and more abiding than their sins. He pleads with them to be at peace with him.

Coming to men through the Bible, God justifies men. He tells them of what he has done through the cross to free them from their guilt. He has removed it; atonement has been made. Guilt no longer exists, separating them from him and bringing upon them the penalties of sin.

Here the Protestant view of justification is different from the Catholic view. For Protestants, justification means that God declares men free from the guilt and penalties of all their sins. That is why he can make their sufferings from sin to be only disciplines, and why he need not punish them in any purgatory. For Catholics, on the other hand, justification begins when God declares men free only from the guilt and penalties of the sin they have inherited from Adam. Hence he does not condemn them to hell. But he continues to hold them guilty and punishable for their own sins, which is why he punishes them in this life and in purgatory. Then, having relieved men of their condemnation to hell, God institutes justification as a lifelong process through which he infuses into them supernatural life, the heavenly kind of life in contrast to the earthly kind of life. For only when men possess the heavenly kind of life does it become right for them, in a legal sort of way, to be with God in heaven. Protestants, however, know nothing of this kind of justification. When God declares men free from all the guilt and penalties of sin, then he makes them ready for sonship with him both in this life and the next.

Coming to men through the Bible, God adopts men as his sons and grants them the blessings of his sons. Sons are adopted when they are taken from other families, and God can be said to adopt men as his sons because he takes them from another family, the family of rebellious men. He adopts them into his own family. Then he bestows upon them the blessings of his sonship, the honor and joy of the sons of God, and eternal life to be with him on both sides of the grave.

Thus God teaches men who are his sons obedience. He does not expect them to be perfect. He is their loving father who understands their weaknesses. Despite their temper tantrums, their impudence, their recurring disobediences, he never disowns them. He sends them to their rooms where they experience the loneliness of partial removal from him; he deprives them of lesser privileges; he allows them to suffer the bruises and the sadness brought upon them both by their own mistakes and the imperfections of the world. But these are not his penalties; these are his disciplines. " For the Lord disciplines him whom he loves." (Heb. 12:6) Persistently, tenderly, he teaches them the perfect obedience that becomes the sons of God.

Here Protestants look at sanctification differently from the way Catholics do. For Protestants, sanctification means that God gradually teaches his sons obedience. In this way he gradually makes them holy, or sanctifies them. For to be holy is to obey God. For Catholics, on the other hand, sanctification means that God gradually infuses into men supernatural life, the heavenly kind of life. In this way he gradually makes them holy, or sanctifies them. For to be holy is to have the supernatural life of heaven. And only after they have that supernatural life are they the kind of beings fit for life in heaven. So long as they have only natural life, the earthly kind of life, they cannot live where the inhabitants have a supernatural kind of life. Protestants, however, do not find this kind of sanctification in the Bible. God makes men holy simply by teaching them obedience, and he teaches them that both in this life and the next.

Since God speaks through the Bible for men's salvation, Protestants call the Bible the primary means of saving grace. God's saving grace or love is his loving work for men's salvation. The Bible is a means of saving grace because God now works through the Bible for men's salvation at every step. The Bible is the primary means of saving grace because God confronts men first through the Bible, there speaking directly to them. God also speaks through secondary means of grace. He speaks through these secondary means because, through the Bible, he has given them their authority and message. In other words, he has set them apart as other ways by which he speaks to men to save them.

The chief secondary means of grace are the two sacraments instituted by Christ, Baptism and the Lord's Supper, and prayer. Through the symbolism of the water of Baptism, and the bread and the wine at the Lord's Supper, God speaks to men of salvation. When adults are baptized, God declares to them that they are cleansed from their guilt, raised with Christ to life eternal, and admitted to sonship with God in the church. When infants are baptized, God declares to their parents that, because the parents are his sons, he counts their children also to be his sons until they reject him. When men, after their baptism, join in the Lord's Supper, God declares to them that through Christ he suffered for their salvation, but now he lives with them, giving them eternal life. And finally, when men pray, God makes men receptive to his coming through the other means of grace, the Bible and the sacraments.

The Protestant interpretation of the means of saving grace is not the same as the Catholic. In the Catholic view, means of saving grace bring men supernatural life. They are the seven sacraments instituted, Catholics believe, by Christ to serve as vehicles or channels by which God transmits to men sanctifying grace, the divine power by which God infuses into men supernatural life. These are: Baptism, the Lord's Supper or Holy Communion, confirmation, penance, marriage, holy orders, and extreme unction. Then there are the means by which the sanctifying grace of the sacraments is increased: prayer, and the sacramentals instituted by the Catholic Church like the rosary, holy water, religious medals, and genuflections.

Protestants do not discover the Catholic view in the Bible, directly or indirectly. To them it suggests that God includes in his work of salvation a mechanical or impersonal process, whereas the Bible everywhere shows that God comes to men to save them in a highly personal way. It is true that for some Protestants the sacraments, besides setting forth God's work of salvation, also bring with them divine power by which God cleanses and strengthens them to do his will. But the power does not impart supernatural life; and men are still justified and sanctified by faith.

Moreover, Protestants believe, the Catholic view, contrary to the Bible, confines God's work of salvation too much to the Catholic Church. Certainly all men do not have to be Catholics to be saved. But God's work of salvation is essentially performed through the Catholic Church through its sacraments. These bring its people spiritual help and blessings not enjoyed by others. Protestants, on the other hand, say that God's work of salvation is essentially performed through the Bible. The Bible alone is necessary. Salvation, therefore, is salvation solely through the Bible, not salvation through the sacraments of the Catholic Church.

III

Thirdly, what must men do to be saved? Protestants answer: Men must simply give up to God and accept his offer of sonship, with all that goes along with it.

This is to be said at once: Whatever men do to be saved depends upon the work of the Holy Spirit within them. As God offers men salvation, he sends into them the Holy Spirit to create the proper responses. If men choose, they can reject the Holy Spirit by destroying what indicates the Spirit's work within them, their impulses to respond to God's offer. But when men allow those impulses to stay alive, then the Holy Spirit brings to maturity the things men do to be saved.

The first and basic thing men do is to have faith. To be saved, men accept God's offer of salvation. But they cannot accept God's salvation at any single point unless they believe God. This is what they do through faith. By faith they believe God when he says that he has worked out their salvation in the past and offers it in the present. Their faith is more than a rational faith, the simple belief that salvation is true. Their faith is a trusting faith, the belief that salvation is true because they have confidence in God who makes it true.

By faith, then, men repent. This is their response to God when he calls them from their rebelliousness. By faith they believe God when he points them to the cross. God loves them! The proof of God's love is that cross silhouetted against a storm-swept world with a man hanging from it and crying out in the agony of rejection and loneliness and suffering, " It is finished." Before that sight their rebellion ceases, and they respond in love. In love they sorrow for their sins, not sorrowing for what sin has done to them, but with sorrow for what sin has done to

God. And then they repent by changing their minds. The English word " repent " translates the Greek New Testament word meaning " to change one's mind." Repenting, men change their minds about trying in self-sufficiency and waywardness to run their own lives apart from God. They stop fighting God and make peace with him.

By faith men accept justification. This is their response to God when he tells them that they are justified. By faith they believe God when he tells them that he took away the guilt and penalties of their sin upon the cross. They know that they are justified; they feel that they are justified. The burden of guilt no longer oppresses them; the fear of penalties is gone. And the burden and the fear never return because all the guilt and all the penalties are no more. This, their justification, is on their side by faith. They do not earn it; they simply accept it, trusting God as he says that he has justified them.

By faith men accept sonship with God, with all its blessings. This is their response to God when he offers to adopt them as his sons. By faith they believe him when he offers it, though to them who have known so much of rebellion and guilt it seems inconceivable. The God of glorious sovereignty would have them be his sons? And along with sonship he offers them eternal life? But they take him at his word. They accept his authority. They become his sons. They experience the honor and joy of being his sons. They have eternal life.

By faith men submit themselves to God's instructions. This is their response to God as he teaches them, his sons, obedience. They accept their sufferings, for whatever cause, as disciplines or instructions. They grow to know his mind and to do his will, and more and more they become the sons of God that they ought to be.

As Protestants see it, men can only accept salvation as the free gift of God's love. In no way does God condition his offer of salvation upon penalties men endure or good works men perform. There are no penalties for men to endure — they have been taken away by the cross. There are no good works men can perform — their best works are imperfect. Under the creative influence of the Holy Spirit men can only accept, honestly and thankfully, the salvation God lovingly provides.

There is, therefore, no place in the Protestant understanding of salvation for two Catholic conceptions, those of penance and merit. Informed Protestants realize that, as Catholics see it, penance and merit do not contradict the fact that salvation is the free gift of God's love. In Catholic opinion, God observes that, were God to require men to do nothing, they would count both him and his salvation cheap. So, he asks of them works of penance and merit which cannot earn salvation for them but which help them to obtain it. To Protestants, however, this seems to be an un-Biblical view that only increases the problems of saving men. Men need to be saved from trying to rule their own lives; but to be told that they can contribute to their salvation through penance and merit only encourages them in the delusion that they can be masters of their fate and captains of their souls. Of course, Protestants recognize that Catholics depend humbly upon God. But it seems to Protestants that this is despite their penitential system, and because of their genuine appreciation that salvation, fundamentally, is solely the gift of God's love.

In rejecting the idea of merit, Protestants also reject the idea that other persons — the Virgin Mary, saints, and ordinary people — can help men to be saved by gaining merit in their behalf. Protestants honor all those who do good, including the saints and the Virgin Mary. But Protestants believe their good deeds to be simply examples of Christian devotion, not means of winning merit for others. In the Protestant view, if transferable merits are to be talked about at all, one must talk about the merits of Jesus Christ. But to do so is not to suggest a merit system.

It is only to suggest that men are saved solely by the work of God through Christ, and not at all by themselves.

Men's answer to God's call to salvation, Protestants emphasize at every point, is personal. Others do not partly answer for them; neither do men submit to the divine authority of a church. In being saved, Catholics submit to the divine authority of the Catholic Church, but Protestants submit to the divine authority of no church. They submit to the authority of God alone as they meet him in the Bible.

Finally, in this section, there is this that is uniquely Protestant: the belief that men can know that they are saved. Catholics hold that only a few Christians, and then by special revelation from God, can be sure of their salvation. Others, by frequent Holy Communions, can merely build up hope. But Protestants hold that Christians can know that they are saved. With the help of the Holy Spirit, they need only trust God as he offers salvation to them through the Bible. Their sure conviction of salvation may come slowly—and to some it comes not at all. But to all it can come, and to many it does come, with the fullness of confidence and joy in God.

IV

Fourthly, what about the possibility of salvation for the various groups of non-Christians? Protestants suggest several answers.

By non-Christians reference is made first to the persons mentioned at the beginning of this chapter's second section, persons who never come to knowledge of salvation through Christ: children dying in infancy, men who lived before Christ, men living after Christ who never heard or hear of him. In addition, reference is made to persons not previously mentioned: those who die knowing but refusing salvation through Christ.

In the Protestant view, all children dying in infancy go

to heaven because they have not begun to rebel against God. In the Catholic view, all baptized infants go to heaven because baptism has infused supernatural life into them, while all unbaptized children go to limbo. Catholic theologians differ about the exact nature of limbo. In general they consider it to be a state happy as compared with the lower levels of hell, but imperfect in happiness as compared with heaven. Since limbo is a place separated from the supernatural life of heaven, it must be regarded as the upper level of hell.

In the Protestant view, God has made salvation possible for persons living before Christ and for persons living after Christ who have never heard of him. What God did through the cross and resurrection of Christ he did for all men. Furthermore, though men never hear of Christ, somehow God makes himself so effectively known to them that they can, if they will, respond to him and be saved. In their own way Catholics agree when they say that such persons can be saved through the baptism of desire, the baptism that follows performance of one perfect act of contrition or repentance. Despite this broad possibility of salvation, both Protestants and Catholics believe Christian missions to be necessary. God comes to men for their salvation most directly, fully, and forcefully through its Christian presentation. Consequently, men are most likely to experience salvation when Christian missions bring it to them.

But what of the destiny of persons who die rejecting God's salvation, no matter how it has been presented to them? Catholics say that they go to hell; and so do most Protestants. They are convinced that persons who die unwilling to be God's sons in this life live on forever apart from God in the next life; and that is the eternal death of hell. But all Protestants wish that somehow God could keep open the possibility of salvation even for those in hell. And some Protestants believe that he does. Indeed, a few but growing number of Protestants believe that God in the overwhelming power of his love will eventually succeed in making all of those in hell to be his sons. If these few Protestants—and one of the greatest of the early Catholic theologians, Origen, who was condemned by the Catholic Church for so believing—are right, then the time will come when there will be none but the sons of God, and God will triumphantly and gloriously conclude his work of salvation.

CHAPTER VI | *Worship*

A venerable Protestant clergyman was telling a meeting of fellow ministers about his recent travels in Europe. He was the most Protestant of them all in the sense that he was probably more quick to express disagreement with Catholics than were any of the others. Yet he told how one Sunday in France, finding himself in a village without a Protestant church, he went to the Catholic church to worship. It was his duty, he felt, to worship God on Sunday with his fellow Christians. And if he could not worship with Protestant fellow Christians, then he would worship with Catholic fellow Christians.

Many Protestants would do the same thing. When unable to worship with Protestants, they are willing to worship with Catholics. Although many Catholic ways of worship are not their ways of worship, they observe that Catholics and Protestants worship the same God in Christ. Consequently they see no wrong in their worshiping with Catholics, adoring God through those forms of Catholic worship meaningful to them, and feeling themselves one in Christ with the Catholics who worship around them.

Of course, Protestants, like Catholics, prefer to worship with others who hold like beliefs and follow familiar forms of worship. Protestants prefer their own forms of worship, because they harmonize with their understanding and expression of Christianity. Just as Catholic forms of worship grow out of and agree with the Catholic conception of Christianity, so Protestant forms of worship grow out of and agree with the Protestant conception of Christianity. And since Protestants believe in their conception of Christianity, they also believe in their Protestant manner of worship.

Protestant worship will be explained in connection with four topics: the nature of worship, helps to worship, the conduct of corporate worship, and the conduct of private worship.

I

First, what is worship? Protestants answer: Worship is paying homage to God.

Ideally, in worship men should render homage to God, acknowledging that God, their Father, in his sovereignty, is their Lord, and they are his people. So one of the psalms calls men to worship: " O come, let us worship and bow down, let us kneel before the Lord, our Maker! For he is our God, and we are the people of his pasture, and the sheep of his hand " (Ps. 95:6-7) . Men can express in several ways the homage to God which is worship: by praising God in his glory and majesty; by thanking him for his goodness, especially for his salvation through Jesus Christ; by confessing their sins to him; by admitting their dependence upon him; and by consecrating themselves to do his will.

Since worship is the rendering of homage to God, worship ought not to be a way by which men try to get what they can from God. Thus seeking their own advantage through worship, men do not render homage to God; they render homage to themselves. Instead of serving God by worship, they set themselves up to be the lords served by worship. Hence men should not worship God to enjoy experiences that are artistically or emotionally satisfying. Nor should they worship God to gain wealth, or friends, or health, or peace, or long life, or any other earthly advantage. In fact, in so far as salvation is to their own advantage rather than expressive of the love of God, men ought not to worship God even to be saved.

But this ideal is too high for men. In their egotism, their childishness, their suffering from the hurts of the world, men do not easily forget themselves. They persist in remembering themselves, and so worship God in greater or smaller measure for their own advantage.

But the loving God who understands the weakness of men adapts himself to their failure to worship him ideally. He accepts even their imperfect worship. Even more, if he deems it for the good of all, now and again he gives them what they ask.

And this Protestants would stress: as God so responds to men's imperfect worship, his response is entirely a gift. Worship is not, as Catholics say, a meritorious work. Men merit no favor for themselves or for others by attending church services, saying prayers, and doing other acts of worship. Worship is simply what they owe God; and in any case, they are God's sinful creatures. God responds to their worship by helping them or others, not because of their merit, but because of his love.

This is what Protestants mean to say when they customarily end their prayers with the phrase, "In Jesus' name." The phrase is no mumbo jumbo by which Protestants would lay hold upon God to make sure he does what they ask. Rather, the phrase is a confession of faith, a confession of faith by which Protestants express their conviction that they can pray confidently to the God who makes himself known in Jesus Christ. He is a loving God; and though they pray imperfectly in their self-seeking, he forgives them, accepts their worship, and ofttime grants them unmerited favors.

Just because God is so marvelous in his love, men should try to forget themselves in worship and think only of him, honoring him not for what he can give them but for what he is in himself. Catholics also know this to be the ideal in worship. It is beautifully expressed for them and for Protestants in a Catholic poem of the seventeenth century, a poem sometimes ascribed to Francis Xavier, and a poem sung by many Protestants as a hymn. The poem reads in part:

> "My God, I love thee; not because
> I hope for heaven thereby,
> Nor yet because who love thee not
> Must die eternally.
>
> . . . .
>
> "Not with the hope of gaining aught,
> Not seeking a reward;
> But as thyself hast loved me,
> O ever-loving Lord!
>
> "E'n so I love thee, and will love,
> And in thy praise will sing;
> Solely because thou art my God,
> And my eternal King."

Because this is ideal worship Protestants pray only to God. They find no Biblical support for the Catholic practice of praying to the Virgin Mary, to saints, and to angels. And such prayer, they believe, makes it more difficult for men to worship God for himself. Of course, for Catholics such prayer is not worship; it is veneration, the expression of a high degree of honor. Still, in the Protestant view, it draws men from ideal worship by emphasizing prayer for personal advantage. Prayer is made to the Virgin, the saints, and the angels chiefly to obtain favors. And the influence of this practice, carrying over to prayer and worship addressed to God, encourages men to worship God for the favors he can give them.

In fact, in the Protestant view, prayer to persons other than God discourages men from worshiping God even for self-seeking reasons. In praying to the Virgin, the saints, and the angels, men look to them for favors as well as to

God. Thus God becomes less important as the supplier of favors. To be sure, Catholics say that the others prayed to can help only through power given them by God. Nevertheless, men tend to become more conscious of them as the immediate answerers of their prayers than they are of the God who enables them to answer. In fact, men tend to forget that God enables them to answer, and credit them with having power in themselves. Thus God more and more fades into the background as the one to be worshiped even for favors.

Protestants join Catholics in saying that worship ought to be continuous. Men ought not to worship God only at one time and in one place. Men ought to worship God at all times and in all places. Worship is not for a moment of life. Worship is to be a way of life in which men continually do homage to God.

II

Secondly, about helps to worship.

Protestants, like Catholics, realize that if men are to worship they need helps. Helps to worship function in two ways. On the one hand, they present God to men so that they can worship him. The cross is an example. The cross speaks to Christians of God's saving work in Christ. Therefore, as they look at it, it speaks to them of God and makes God real or present to them. On the other hand, helps to worship enable men to present themselves to God in worship. The giving of offerings is an example. Through offerings men express their consecration to God and so worship him.

Protestants are more hesitant than Catholics, however, in using as helps to worship such things as crosses, statues of the Christ, pictures, vestments, incense, complex liturgies, prayers read from books, genuflections, holy water, candles, and making the sign of the cross. Helps of this type, Protestants grant, assist many persons to center their attention upon God and address him. But Protestants feel that too many helps of this type can and do become hindrances to worship by diverting men's attention from God. Men easily become preoccupied with them for their own sakes, as traditional, or as beautiful, or as mechanics to be carried out, or as possessing some supernatural power.

Protestant denominations and individuals vary in using helps to worship. Protestants agree that the Bible directly approves six chief helps: reading the Bible, sacraments, preaching, hymns, prayers, and the giving of offerings. But otherwise Protestants think that the Bible allows Christians freedom to employ good sense and taste in developing worship helps as they seem useful, provided they accord with the general teachings of the Bible.

It seems good sense to Protestants that verbal helps to worship should be in the vernacular, the language of the people. Scripture readings, prayer, the liturgy, words of music sung by choirs — these should be in the language worshipers understand. Otherwise God cannot speak to them nor can they speak to him whom they worship. So Protestants have no Latin liturgies as do Catholics.

Protestants, it was just said, look upon six chief helps to worship as being directly approved by the Bible: reading the Bible, sacraments, preaching, hymns, prayers, and the giving of offerings. The reading of the Bible is fundamental since the Bible immediately presents God. The other five helps to worship become helps as, authorized and given meaning by the Bible, they too present God.

The six chief helps to worship also enable the worshipers to appear before God. Through them worshipers make known to God their sentiments in worship, such as praise, thanksgiving, confession, and consecration. Thus, for example, by listening receptively to the Bible and preaching, worshipers can praise God; by participating in services of the sacraments, worshipers can thank God for making them his sons; through prayers they can confess their sins to God; through hymns and offerings they can express their devotion to God.

Protestants do not worship God through the Sacrifice of the Mass, which to Catholics is the most important part of worship. In the Sacrifice of the Mass, Christ is slain again in an unbloody sacrifice that continues his sacrifice upon the cross. This continuing sacrifice makes available the supererogatory merits won by Christ and the saints, the merits they did not need for themselves, and which make possible men's salvation to heaven. For Protestants, however, there can be no continuing Sacrifice of the Mass because Christ, dying once upon the cross, completed his sacrifice.

Moreover, unlike Catholics, Protestants do not worship by adoring the Host. In Catholic worship the Host is the bread of the Eucharist which, by the action of the Mass, becomes the veritable body of Christ as at the same time the wine of the Eucharist, by the same action, becomes the veritable blood of Christ. This is the process known as transubstantiation. Catholic congregations adore the Host as Christ himself. And a portion of the Host is reserved, or left upon the altar, so that individual Catholics can make their devotions before it. Also, the Host is sometimes carried in outdoor religious processions to be adored by the faithful. Protestants find nothing of this sort approved by the Bible. It seems to them that it easily leads to something close to idolatry—and actually does in some cases, and to the forgetting that Christ is everywhere and can be worshiped anywhere.

III

Thirdly, Protestant conduct of corporate worship, the worship in which they meet to worship as congregations.

Ordinarily Protestants meet for worship on Sunday, or on the Sabbath, as some prefer to say. To use a Catholic phrase, Sunday is the one holy day of obligation observed by Protestants. For them Sunday is the only day set apart in the Bible as a day on which Christians, turning aside from their ordinary occupations, should give special time and attention to congregational worship. So Protestants do not have numerous other holydays of obligations as Catholics do, such as the Feast of the Ascension and the Feast of the Assumption. They do appoint special days of prayer. They do more or less follow the Christian year, with its days and seasons remembering the life of Christ. Particularly, they emphasize Sundays like Christmas Sunday and Whitsunday (Pentecost), and weekdays like Ash Wednesday and Good Friday. And they do designate Sundays of special interest to Protestants, like Reformation Sunday and Bible Sunday. But their observance of these days is voluntary and greatly varied.

Protestant emphasis on Sunday leads many Protestants, especially those in Britain and America, to a strict keeping of Sunday, or the Sabbath. Although Catholics look upon Sunday as the principal day for worship and rest, they regard recreation as a form of rest, and freely engage in all kinds of commercial and noncommercial Sunday amusements. A fairly sizable number of Protestants oppose Sunday amusements, especially Sunday commercial amusements. For them the Bible intends that Sunday should be a day of rest not only from work but also from recreation. These Protestants are rapidly becoming fewer and less strict. But their influence sustains among British and American Protestants uneasiness lest Sunday be lived with too much frivolity and concern for money-making, and too little regard for rest and worship.

On Sundays most Protestant churches hold several types of corporate worship services. There are Sunday church schools, usually in the morning and usually for all ages, during which classes and departments meet for worship and study of Christian matters, especially the Bible. There are young people's meetings, usually in the evening and usually for junior and senior high schoolers, during which young people gather for worship, study, and fellowship. In addition there are the main congregational services of Sunday worship, the preaching services and the services of the sacraments.

Protestant churches have Sunday morning preaching services except for the occasions when they celebrate the Holy Communion. Ordinarily the services are held at ten thirty or eleven o'clock after the church school periods. Some Protestant churches also have Sunday evening preaching services. Both morning and evening services last about an hour, and follow much the same pattern. Though they vary somewhat from denomination to denomination, and from congregation to congregation, all include the six chief helps to worship. Preaching takes up the most time, with sermons lasting from twenty to thirty minutes. In entering their sanctuaries, Protestants do not, like Catholics, touch their fingers in holy water, make the sign of the cross, or genuflect before they take their seats. Sometimes, just after they take their seats, they do bow in silent prayer.

The entire congregation takes part in the service of worship. There is considerable use of responsive readings, readings in which the minister and the congregation alternate in reading passages from the Bible, usually from The Psalms. Usually choirs of both men and women help congregations with the singing of the hymns, and sing anthems and responses. Occasionally there are junior choirs of children. Most congregations say the "Our Father," and often congregations pray unison prayers of confession of sins. Quite a number of congregations recite the Apostles' Creed.

A Protestant preaching service is conducted by someone appointed either by the denomination or by the local church. Usually he is a clergyman, and usually he leads the different parts of the service and preaches a sermon. Sometimes, however, a layman may do everything a clergyman does, or simply assist the clergyman. A clergyman who presides at the congregational worship of his parish does so as the pastor and teacher of the congregation.

In conducting worship services, Protestant clergymen wear a variety of dress. Some wear ordinary suits to indicate that they do not belong to a priestly class different from that of the people. Some wear simple black robes to suggest their teaching office. Some wear clerical collars to show that they have been ordained, not to a separate priestly class, but to a particular office within the church. Some, like Catholic priests, change their vestments with the progressing days of the Christian year to remind their congregations of the different events in the life of Christ.

Protestants ordinarily celebrate their two sacraments, Baptism and the Lord's Supper, on designated Sundays with the whole congregation present. Baptism and Communion are conducted in private ceremonies only for some special reason such as the illness of those receiving the sacraments. Even then laymen often go with the clergymen to represent their congregations. Ordinarily the Lord's Supper is held at least four times a year, but some Protestants observe it every Sunday. Baptism sometimes is held in connection with the Lord's Supper. In the Holy Communion the entire congregation meets as a Christian family — God's sons — around the Table of its Lord. In Baptism the congregation pledges itself to help in the Christian growth of the one baptized.

Protestant denominations generally allow only clergymen to administer their sacraments. In a few denominations, if clergymen are not available, congregations may appoint laymen to lead in the celebration of the Holy Communion. Protestant clergymen always administer Baptism. In Catholic practice, of course, if the person to be baptized may die before a priest can come, any lay person, including a Catholic, Protestant, or pagan, can perform the

Baptism provided he does so in the name of the Trinity and intends to perform a Catholic Baptism. Protestant laymen, however, may assist clergymen in the baptismal service, for example, by holding the vessel containing the water. And during the Holy Communion, they may pass the bread and wine from the clergymen to the people.

Most Protestant denominations baptize by sprinkling water on the head, which differs from Catholic baptism by laving, or allowing water to flow upon the head. Like the Catholic Church, most Protestant denominations baptize both infants and adults. Some Protestant denominations administer Baptism only to adults, or those come to the age of personal responsibility; and they baptize by immersion, submerging the individual completely under water. Protestant parents take their children for Baptism within a few weeks after birth, but they feel no sense of haste, since Protestants believe that even unbaptized infants go to heaven should they die.

Generally speaking, Protestant denominations receive persons whom they baptize into membership as baptized members. Adults are at the same time received both as baptized members and as communing members, members with the right to take Communion. Infants or small children are not immediately received as communing members. In later years, when they are old enough to know their own minds, they decide whether they want to become communing members. While they remain only baptized members, some Protestant denominations regard them as members in a real but incomplete way, and other Protestant churches regard them as provisional or temporary members.

Usually Protestants serve the Holy Communion only to the communing members of the church. Most Protestant churches invite all communing members of any denomination or congregation to commune with them. Only a few Protestant churches restrict Communion to their own membership and the number is declining. Most Protestants accept the invitation of any church to its Communion. Some Protestants, however, believe that they should commune only when Communion is celebrated by clergymen of their own denomination.

In communing, Protestant churches usually serve bread and unfermented grape juice. In some denominations the congregation remains in the pews to receive the bread and wine from laymen who bring them from the presiding clergymen. In other denominations the worshipers go to the front of the church in small groups to receive the bread and wine from the clergymen. Sometimes the bread is torn from a single loaf and the wine is served from a common cup, but usually the bread is brought to the service in small pieces and the wine in small, individual glasses. In some churches, worshipers go to the front to receive the wine by intinction, in which the clergyman dips the bread, usually in the form of a wafer, into a cup of wine and then places it on the tongue of the communicant.

Protestant laymen " commune in both kinds." Catholic laymen commune in one kind, taking only the bread. In Protestant churches, therefore, the presiding clergymen, unlike Catholic priests, are not alone in taking the wine. This is partly because for Protestants the Communion is a congregational experience, partly because Protestants, not believing that the wine becomes the blood of Christ, are not afraid lest it be profaned by the spilling of some of it, and partly because Protestants believe that the Bible teaches communion in both kinds.

Protestants are not gravely concerned about what happens to bread and wine left over from Holy Communion. Catholic priests take special pains to dispose of remaining bread and wine, since they have become the actual body and blood of Christ. Priests will give their lives to save the Host from profanation, as by fire in a burning church building. Protestants, not so believing about the bread and wine, think that after the bread and wine have served their symbolic purpose, they should be disposed of in a dignified, but ordinary way.

In addition to their preaching and sacramental services, Protestants, of course, hold funeral services. Almost always the services are conducted by clergymen. They are held sometimes in private homes, sometimes in church sanctuaries, and increasingly in funeral homes when such places are available. Usually they are attended only by the family and friends of the deceased. Protestants seldom refuse to hold funeral services for other Protestants and non-Protestants, including even non-Christians. And all Protestants bury all persons in the same cemeteries. In the Protestant view, at death men are one in their common need of depending solely upon God in his love to give them their proper places in the hereafter. At the same time, those who remain behind need to be reminded of that fact. So when men die, Protestants are not inclined to make distinctions among them by burying some in consecrated or holy ground, and some in unconsecrated ground.

IV

Fourthly, about the conduct of private worship. How do Protestants worship, not as congregations, but as individuals or as small groups of individuals?

Protestants believe that private worship can be performed as effectively outside church sanctuaries as it can be inside them. Since they do not believe that Christ remains upon the altar in the form of the Host, they emphasize the fact that Christ is everywhere. And since Christ is everywhere, men can worship him as well outside church sanctuaries as they can inside them. On the other hand, individual Protestants do sometimes go into church sanctuaries to worship because they are places of quiet apart from the rush and noise of the world.

Protestants worship alone in their rooms, before they go

to bed, or on rising and during the day. They worship around the family table, saying grace before meals or joining in family worship. They worship in the office and the factory, on the farm and in the mines. Unfortunately, Protestants are not equally faithful in such worship. But many of them turn to God wherever they are.

Family worship is given special stress among Protestants. They agree with Catholics that " the family that prays together stays together." And they believe that during the week the home is to be a sanctuary where the family can gather for its own worship. The family may worship after a meal, or before going to bed at night. Scripture may be read, or perhaps devotional material. Prayers may be said, hymns sung, the Christian life discussed. Thus the family worships as a kind of Christian congregation in miniature.

Protestants are encouraged to frame their own prayers, and many of them do. Protestants realize that reading the prayers of others often helps men pray by putting into words what they cannot say; so they sometimes use the prayers of others. But they also realize that often they can pray most genuinely and freely through their own prayers.

Protestants do not follow many practices common to Catholics. They do not observe the Stations of the Cross, or go on pilgrimages, or adore the Sacred Heart of Jesus, or make novenas, or say indulgenced prayers. They do not keep on their persons, or in their homes, or in their automobiles, blessed objects like medals, scapulars, sacred pictures, holy water, or statues of Jesus, the Virgin, and the saints. Protestants recognize that these can be valuable aids to worship in so far as they help the worshiper to become conscious of the presence of God. But Protestants avoid them. For Protestants, they are not in accord with the Bible, and they easily become objects of a superstitious or idolatrous character that turn the worshiper aside from God.

Protestants do not pray the prayers that for Catholics are

not worship but veneration. Protestants do not say the Rosary, or pray otherwise to the Virgin in her various manifestations. An individual Protestant does not pray to a patron saint or angel — for Protestants there are no saints or angels who are patrons. Nor do Protestants pray to any saint or angel. Again Protestants do not believe that the Bible approves, and they think that such prayers easily turn men from praying to God.

Protestant private worship, compared with Catholic private worship, is plain and unadorned because Protestants believe this agrees with the Bible. The Bible seeks genuine worship, and worship is likely to be more genuine if it is as free as possible from the mechanics and objects of elaborate ritual. Of course, worship does not become genuine simply in freedom from elaborate ritual. Genuine worship requires a heart truly ready to do homage to God. But Protestants find some support for their position in the stark simplicity of the private worship of some Catholic monastic orders such as the Cistercians. And so they would worship God in a plain fashion, reading the Bible, making their own prayers, and helped by the shared experiences of their brethren in the faith. After all, this is the way Jesus worshiped.

CHAPTER VII | *The Christian Life*

How should Christians act? What is proper Christian behavior? What are Christian morals? What, in other words, does it mean for Christians to live good lives? This is the problem of the Christian life. And this is the problem to which the present chapter will give a Protestant answer.

This chapter will answer for Protestantism in a comprehensive way. Then the next chapter will deal with a particular matter of special interest to Catholics and Protestants, Christian marriage. Here the Christian life will be discussed broadly under three heads: the nature, the basic lessons, and the larger lessons of the Christian life.

I

First, the nature of the Christian life. What does it mean for Christians to lead good lives, or to be good men? Protestants answer: It means for them to practice the obedience of the sons of God.

Fundamentally, there is no such thing as a good Christian life or a good Christian man. The first reason appears in connection with the only perfect man of the Bible. Jesus said exactly that of himself. A Jewish ruler once addressed him as " Good Teacher." Jesus replied: " Why do you call me good? No one is good but God alone." (Luke 18:18-19.) The second reason appears from the lives of the other men of the Bible. They were all sinful. Even the apostle Paul lamented, " I am the foremost of sinners."

(I Tim. 1:15.) Fundamentally, then, there are no good Christians because all men are and remain sinners.

Is there any sense, however, in which Christians can be called good? There is. Jesus gave part of the answer to the Jewish ruler. He said, " No one is good but God alone "; and then he went on to refer to the Ten Commandments through which God spoke to Moses. Men can be called good, Jesus was saying, only if they accept the authority of God. Paul also gave part of the answer. He wrote of himself, " I am the very least of all the saints." (Eph. 3:8.) Sinner though he was, he was yet a saint or good man. And the reason? It appears throughout his entire ministry. He knew that God never ceased to forgive him, and he was a good man because he was a forgiven man. In this sense, then, Christians can be called good: they can be called good through their acceptance of the authority and forgiveness of God.

In other words, Christians can be called good when they are saved to the obedience of the sons of God. Saved to that obedience, they are saved from their own authority to the authority of God. Thus they are saved from lives lived under guilt to lives lived within the forgiveness of God. They are good men because on their side they undertake, however incompletely, to obey the commandments of God, and because on his side God forgives their every failure.

For Protestants, therefore, saints are not what they are for Catholics. As Catholics see them, saints are those who come to perfect obedience, and they are, as one modern Catholic writer has put it humorously, severely rationed. Saints are few! But Protestants believe that though none of God's sons obeys him perfectly, all of God's sons are saints. All Christians become saints in becoming sons of God, which is why Paul so often called the people of his churches saints. Called of God, though imperfect, they pledge themselves to do his will, trusting him to forgive when they fail. They are saints by faith, not by works.

Moreover, think Protestants, since the sons of God are always imperfect, the temporal blessings they experience, the blessings of this earthly life, are the gift of God. Imperfect sons cannot merit them. Thus Protestants differ with Catholics who hold that saved men can merit temporal blessings, life, good fortune, health, friends, and business success. (Incidentally, Protestants also differ with the Catholic view that temporal blessings can be secured through the use of the sacramentals, religious medals, candles, and the rest. To Protestants this seems somewhat superstitious and mechanical.) As Protestants see it, temporal blessings are unmerited favors that God grants his sons according to his knowledge of what is best for them. They can in no way be purchased from him.

Still, the imperfect sons of God seek to obey God more completely. They are not satisfied to accept God's offer of forgiveness and continue in disobedience. By faith and in love they became the sons of God, and by faith and in love they would become the obedient sons of God. By faith they believe God, when, speaking through the Bible, he teaches them what obedience means. In love they continue to submit to his authority, wanting to do his will, seeking out his will, trying to do his will, though they are sometimes more eager and sometimes less eager.

At every step, Protestants think, God helps his sons through the Holy Spirit. The Holy Spirit enables them to respond to God as God teaches them through the Bible. In Catholic thought, God also helps men to perform acts pleasing to him. He does it, however, through actual grace, a divine power secured by prayer, and, on the authority of the Catholic Church, through sacramentals. To Protestants, since the grace comes apart from the personal Word given through the Bible, here again is something approaching the superstitious and the mechanical.

How do the sons of God, desiring to do his will, discover

it? There is development to be noted here. To accept the authority of God is to accept it over all things; and so the sons of God begin by examining themselves and their experiences in connection with what God says in the Bible. Then something happens to them. They feel themselves pushed by their experiences, driven by them, to learn new ways of obeying God. Then it dawns on them that in their experiences there is more than the devisings of men, impersonal nature, chance, or evil. In their experiences is somehow God, seeking to make his will known to them. The God who speaks in the Bible through history continues to speak through history, challenging, goading his sons to know his will. He does not, however, speak apart from the Bible. Speaking through history, he sends his sons to the Bible to hear him speaking there. For only through the guidance of his infallible Word in the Bible can they be sure of what he is saying in history.

In coming to understand God's will in this fashion, the sons of God have a personal encounter with God. He comes to them as person to person, teaching them directly the meaning of obedience. He does not come, Protestants think, through the authority of the Catholic Church to determine and enforce Christian morality. And as he comes he sometimes addresses all of his sons, sometimes groups of them, and sometimes individuals among them. This personal encounter of the sons of God with their Father has important bearings upon their learning of obedience.

Since God teaches them as person to person, his sons must keep themselves open to whatever new he has to say. He gives them certain general principles to follow, and he expects them to work out some things for themselves. But as new situations demand new answers, and as their ability to make answer varies with their knowledge and experience, like all fathers with their sons, God teaches them new ways of obedience. Not that he contradicts his earlier instructions. Rather, he brings out more fully and clearly and exactly what he intended at the time. Moreover, thus learning new ways of obedience, the sons of God also grow in what itself is a way of obedience, humility toward God. They discover that they don't know it all, and by themselves can't know it all!

It is therefore important, Protestants believe, for the sons of God to avoid what is called, in technical theological terms, the obediences of legalism, rationalism, and moralism. All three types of obedience help to keep the sons of God from hearing their Father speak to them personally. Legalistic obedience is obedience to completed and unchangeable divine laws; obeying them the sons of God think that he has nothing more to say. Rationalistic obedience is obedience to deductions made from a general body of knowledge, including divine laws; obeying them the sons of God conclude that they can think out his will without further word from him. Moralistic obedience is obedience given to a select type of action; obeying it men imagine that God has no other action of which to tell them. And all three types of obedience foster pride: legalistic obedience by encouraging men to think that they know it all, that God has said everything he has to say; rationalistic obedience by encouraging them to think that they *can* know it all, that they can figure out God's will for themselves; moralistic obedience by encouraging them to think that they know at least one thing for sure, that on this one thing there can be no other way of obeying God.

It is easy indeed for the sons of God to fall into these errors. Certainly Protestants do not completely avoid them. Sometimes they forget that God speaks anew, and sometimes their pride traps them. Some Protestants are given to a negative moralism once more prevalent among Protestants than it is now, the negative moralism that binds Christians to obey God by totally abstaining from things like tobacco, cards, dancing, drinking, and the theater. And Protestants fear that Catholics, for their part, are especially susceptible to legalism and rationalism—for example, Catholic casuistry, a moral science by which from a set of divine laws experts in casuistry deduce answers to questions of moral conduct.

The personal encounter with God by which his sons learn obedience confronts all of them, and this too has important bearings upon their learning of obedience. For one thing, the sons of God learn obedience together. God speaks to them in groups where they share their experiences and study the Bible together. For the second thing, the sons of God are equally responsible for obedience to the whole will of God. None of them is more responsible than the others for obedience. At this point Protestants differ from Catholics. For Catholics there are evangelical counsels, the chief among them being absolute poverty, chastity, and obedience, binding only upon those who choose to make them binding, for example, the men and women of the religious orders, the monastics and the nuns. Protestants, however, think it improper for the sons of God to decide which of their Father's commandments they should obey.

Still, Protestants recognize, God himself may charge particular groups or individuals with special obligations. God in his personal encounter with groups and individuals may approach some with particular commandments not laid by him upon others. Protestant pacifists are an example. God makes such persons no better or more honored than others. He simply makes them responsible for a special duty.

This is the final and tremendous thing about the disobedience of the sons of God: it is unafraid! The sons of God are conscious of their awful responsibility to obey God, on the one hand, and their failure to obey God perfectly on the other hand. So fearful is this predicament that it would paralyze them with terror were it not for one thing: " There is therefore now no condemnation for those who are in Christ Jesus" (Rom. 8:1). God forgives! He has saved them from the guilt and penalties of their rebellion, and he saves them from any guilt and penalties on account of their continuing disobedience. So they can obey him freely, unafraid of the inevitable mistakes. In faith and love toward God who loves them, they need only do their best and keep on trying to do their best.

II

Secondly, the basic lessons of the Christian life. What are the fundamental lessons that the sons of God must learn in order to obey their Father? Protestants answer: They learn five such lessons from him who was the perfect Son of God, Jesus Christ. For through the incarnation there was such a combining of God and man that men can see in Christ not only how God acts toward them but how a perfect son obeys his Father.

1. Through Christ men learn the meaning of absolute obedience to God, the complete obedience that allows nothing to come between them and God. The sons of God purpose to render God this kind of obedience when they accept his authority. But they learn from Christ the things to be avoided if they are actually to render absolute obedience.

The sons of God must not allow life to come between themselves and God; if necessary, they must be willing to die as Christ died. They must not allow people and things to come between themselves and God; Jesus left his home and possessions. Nor must they allow the desire for rewards to come between themselves and God; Jesus died on a cross. The sons of God must not allow laziness to come between themselves and God: Jesus said, "My Father is working still, and I am working" (John 5:17).

2. Through Christ men learn how they are to love other men.

The sons of God must love all their fellow men; Christ

came to all. They must serve the needs of others; Christ went about doing good. They must be humble before others; Christ washed the disciples' feet. And they must forgive others; Christ died saying, " Father, forgive them; for they know not what they do " (Luke 23:34). The sons of God must expect nothing from others; Christ asked nothing from others — not even their love. That cannot be asked; it can only be given.

3. Through Christ the sons of God learn how to understand the commandments of the Old Testament.

Jesus dealt with this matter in the Sermon on the Mount. (Matt., ch. 5.) He had come, he said, not to abolish the Old Testament commandments, but to fulfill them. Then he went on to warn against the righteousness of the Pharisees whose obedience to the Old Testament commandments was shot through with legalism and rationalism. One cannot, Jesus showed, only obey the law exactly as it stands, which is legalism; nor can one, apart from life's experiences, deduce from it what one ought to do, which is rationalism. To obey the law properly one must see its wider reference in the light of experiences not mentioned by the letter of the law itself.

Jesus gave several examples of what he meant. The first had to do with murder. There is, said Jesus, the Old Testament commandment, " You shall not kill; and whoever kills shall be liable to judgment." But suppose a person becomes angry. Then in his anger he can't see that the commandment applies to more than killing a man physically; it also applies to being angry at a man. For what is anger? Anger is really a form of killing. At the least an angry man kills another by not allowing him to talk: he forces the other to keep quiet and therefore become essentially dead. At the worst an angry man would kill another man if he dared or could; he kills the other man in his own mind. Consequently, anger is a form of murder, and the commandment, " You shall not kill," applies to it.

No wonder Jesus said that he came not to destroy but to fulfill the commandments! Approached in this way they become much more sweeping in their reference.

Then Jesus did something else to show how the Old Testament commandments are to be understood. At first it looks as though he set aside some of the commandments. He said: " You have heard that it was said, ' An eye for an eye and a tooth for a tooth.' But I say to you, Do not resist one who is evil. . . . You have heard that it was said, ' You shall love your neighbor and hate your enemy.' But I say to you, Love your enemies and pray for those who persecute you." (Matt. 5:38-39, 43-44.)

Surprisingly, Jesus was simply fulfilling the old laws. He was making explicit the love to which God pointed through them. Originally they were given to men who recognized no limit to revenge and who hated even their neighbors. So when they were told to limit themselves to an eye for an eye and a tooth for a tooth, and to extend their love to their neighbors, God was bringing them one step along the way to love that takes no revenge and loves even enemies. It was of this love that Jesus spoke. In speaking of it, he was not setting aside the old commandments: they were still applicable to men at a lower level of moral development. Instead, he was making clear the full meaning of the love that the commandments partially express and to which they point. And in similar fashion, he was saying that the sons of God should examine many old commandments. Through their fuller knowledge of the love of God, they should discover what God was saying in commandments that in themselves may seem untrue to the purpose of a loving God.

4. Through Christ, the sons of God learn how suffering disciplines.

It is not easy for men to realize that suffering is discipline. They know that God saves them from the penalties of sin, but since they also know how their continuing disobedience hurts their Father, repeatedly a sense of guilt comes upon them. They hardly dare believe that his chastisements are the judgments of a loving father who would warn and teach his children, and therefore quite different from the judgments of a judge who penalizes a criminal. It is then that the sons of God find assurance through Christ. Before them stands his cross as the abiding proof of their forgiveness. And again and again they are persuaded by that cross that their sufferings are not penalties after all.

At the same time, the sons of God are constantly reminded through Christ that their sufferings are disciplines. Says The Epistle to the Hebrews: In Christ we have not one "unable to sympathize with our weaknesses, but one who in every respect has been tempted as we are, yet without sin. . . . Although he was a Son, he learned obedience through what he suffered" (chs. 4:15; 5:8). Through suffering, Christ learned the humility, patience, selflessness, and constancy which are obedience to God. And so can the sons of God.

5. Through Christ men learn to accept special vocations. The obedience of Christ was a special vocation, a particular responsibility laid upon him by his Father. To Pilate he said, "For this was I born, and for this I have come into the world, to bear witness to the truth." (John 18:37.) God had given him a unique work to do, and it was for him to do it. He never asked others to do what was especially appointed to him. Of course, he taught them to follow his general example, but in their areas of life, not in his. God had called him, not them, to be the savior of the world. That was his special obligation, and his alone.

But the sons of God, observing the example of Jesus, need always to keep themselves open to some special task from God. Does he want them to fight bravely for him, or because of him to refuse to fight? Does he want them to marry or not to marry? Does he want them to be Christian laymen or Christian clergymen? The sons of God should examine the demands of their immediate situation; they should examine their own personal qualities and responsibilities. Then, confronting the God of the Bible, they should ask whether he has a special vocation for them. If he does, they are to accept it, humbly and to the end, whatever that may be.

III

And now, thirdly, the larger lessons of the Christian life. By these are meant the lessons of the Christian life relating to Christian social concern. This is the obedience owed by the sons of God in matters affecting the lives of people as they live together in large social groups beyond the family, such as those in factories, in other races and nations. Here four of today's chief social problems are chosen for discussion to illustrate the Protestant position on social obedience, race, economic justice, peace, and world order.

Certainly Protestants must pay tribute to the Catholic Church for its Christian social concern. The social encyclicals and other statements of recent popes have been outstandingly influential around the world, and they continue to be studied by many Catholic priests and laymen. In various places Catholic bishops are taking a forthright stand on race issues. Individual Catholic priests and laymen on water fronts, in factories, on farms, in unions, and in labor schools are doing much to forward economic justice; and, of course, American Catholics have a Catholic labor union. A few Catholic pacifists witness eloquently for peace among the nations by voluntarily accepting pacifism as their special Christian obligation. Catholic statements contribute much to more effective political relations among the nations, that is, a world order more favorable to racial and economic justice and to peace.

Protestants have their own sense of Christian social concern. Protestants, like Catholics, are sometimes more concerned, sometimes less concerned. But as a whole Protestants are moving forward. Protestant denominations make regular social pronouncements and encourage their members to social study and action. Three smaller groups, the Mennonites, Friends, and Church of the Brethren have always advocated pacifism as the general teaching of Jesus. Individuals of other denominations also adopt pacifism either as a general duty or as a special obligation laid upon them by God. In the United States the Protestant National Council of Churches, and in the world the World Council of Churches to which most Protestant denominations belong, promote social study and carry on service projects. Through the World Council and sometimes through their own denominations directly Protestants are doing much for the world's war refugees. Protestant young people volunteer for nonpaid summer relief work at home and abroad. Protestant businessmen, labor leaders, and statesmen, as well as Protestants in less strategic positions, seek to discover and do God's social will in the places where they are responsible.

But Catholics and Protestants are not the only ones interested in social problems and, more particularly, in the four specific problems to be considered now: race, economic justice, peace, and world order. All the people of the world are interested, and the Communists are especially interested! There is no color line among Communists, and they pursue economic justice, peace, and world order, albeit in their own way. Indeed, it seems to Protestants, at least, that the people of the world are often more interested than Protestants and Catholics in solving these social problems. What is the explanation? In so far as there are those among the peoples of the world who are not the sons of God, the words of Jesus apply. Often, said Jesus, "the sons of this world are wiser in their own generation than the sons of light" (Luke 16:8). Often, responding to the events of these days, the sons of men are wiser than the sons of God.

The events of these days which raise the problems of race, economic justice, peace, and world order are faced by both the sons of men and the sons of God. There are the events relating to race: the rise of the darker peoples in education and political power, the living of large numbers of them in the same areas with whites. Other events relate to economic justice: developments in science and industry leading on the one hand to labor problems, and on the other hand to the possibility of more food, more clothing, more automobiles — more of everything for more men everywhere. Still others are the events relating to peace: two world wars not to mention several small wars, new means of mass slaughter, racial and national unrest, economic competition among nations. And finally, there are the events relating to world order: all manner of conflict among nations big and little, the search for some kind of international organization that can control unruly nations as nations control unruly individuals.

In the face of the events of these days the sons of men become wise according to their intention. The sons of men propose to run their own lives apart from the authority of God. But, they realize, the running of their own lives requires a certain amount of live and let live. To get what they want, they need the help of others, so they make all men, without regard to race, their comrades or their associates in the business of getting. To keep what they have or get, they must keep others content; so they further the cause of economic justice by providing others with an ample supply of things. To run their own lives, they must remain alive; so they seek peace. To protect themselves and their possessions, they seek an arrangement to keep the nations in line; so they favor some kind of assemblage of nations.

How wise are the sons of men — and yet how unwise! They are rebels against God: so they think themselves alive when they are already dead in the death which is eternal. They have comrades, associates in work, not brothers in the family of God; so they are tool-making animals in a loveless world. If others refuse to help them or get in their way, they hate them and would destroy them;

so they are violent people who periodically go to war themselves or incite others to war, and in the process destroy for everyone what their economic justice has brought.

Through the events of these days, however, the sons of God are summoned to a higher wisdom, the wisdom which is the obedience of the sons of God. The events of these days are not a mere series of circumstances. In the providence of God they are circumstances that are calling the sons of God to a further understanding of his will. Thus called, they are impelled to go to the Bible where God speaks through his Word. So to the Bible they go, there to learn the obedience of the sons of God in present areas of Christian social concern.

Through the Bible, God declares to them his will about race, economic justice, peace, and world order. Upon the cross he acted for all and equally; so it is clear that God wills racial and economic equality for all men equally. Upon the cross he acted to bring peace between himself and men; so it is clear that God wills peace among men. Upon the cross he acted to extend his authority over men completely; so it is clear that he wills a world order in which the nations will recognize his authority. All these things God wills, and his sons must carry out their Father's will. He does not tell them, however, by what social procedures or organizations they are to put his will into effect. These he makes them responsible for according to their wisdom and the changing circumstances of society.

But God does give his sons some basic general instructions about the achievement of his social objectives. Their complete achievement requires that men become the perfect sons of God; for only then will they completely do his will. Hence, to bring in the Father's will, his sons should seek to call all men first to become the sons of God, and then to become better sons. Meanwhile, however, the many, many sons of men remain. Obedient only to their own will, they follow the wisdom of the world that leads to the precarious adjustments among men in which they will to live and let live. Hence the sons of God, to serve their Father's will, should urge the sons of men to pursue zealously their own wisdom in order to achieve all the racial and economic justice, peace, and security in world order that such wisdom can bring. This accords with Jesus' recognition of the need of a lower law for men at a lower level of morality.

But the sons of God cannot hear their Father's message with personal satisfaction. They realize their shortcomings in social disobedience. They contribute to racial and economic injustice; they do not act in love toward their enemies as they should; they are negligent in working for a better world order. And their shame increases when they observe the sons of men. Wise according to their wisdom, the sons of men do much for godless reasons that the sons of God should do for godly reasons — and sometimes more. Shamed, the sons of God confess that the social difficulties of the world result in part from their failures. And shamed, the sons of God recognize that their failures bring upon them the sufferings of discipline. Some of these sufferings they bring upon themselves. Others come from the sins of the sons of men.

So it is, Protestants believe, that the sons of God should look upon Communists and be shamed. Communists deny God, but often they are more actively concerned than the sons of God for racial and economic justice, and peace and world order. Denying God, the Communists sometimes do what the sons of God, affirming God, ought to do but do not do. And what is more, the sons of God must accept sufferings brought upon them by the evils of communism as disciplines of God designed to impress them with their social failures and to move them to social action. Certainly the sons of God must pray for Communists, seeking their conversion to sonship with God. But certainly also the sons of God must pray for themselves, confessing both their personal social sins and their group social sins when gathered together as the church, and asking God to bring them to greater social obedience.

How successful will the sons of God be in building a better world? God speaking through the Bible gives them little encouragement. Good will increase — the Kingdom grows, said Jesus. But evil will also increase — there will be wars and rumors of wars until the end, said Jesus; and men will wax more evil (II Tim. 3:13). Within less than a half century the world recently experienced two world wars, sure signs of the sins by which men shatter every social order, however just. And the prospect of yet more terrible world wars is a fearful one. The gospel has won more men to sonship with God than ever before, but the sons of men are also multiplying. And the many sons of God are far from perfect. If a better world depends upon the good works or the merit of men, there is little hope.

But the Bible leaves the sons of God with great hope. There will be a perfect world, a world in which social evils will be no more. And it will be the gift of God. This is the meaning of the Second Coming of Christ. Here God speaks through the Bible in symbols sometimes impossible to understand fully, but his essential message is plain enough. Through Christ he came first to inaugurate his Kingdom, his rule over his sons, as a gift. Through Christ he will come again to complete his Kingdom as a gift — sometime, somehow. The Kingdom comes in fullness from above. It is given, the sons of men neither achieving nor deserving it. Only the Father himself knows the time of its coming or just how it will come. But it will come. It will come because God has promised it. And when it comes there will be " a new earth in which righteousness dwells " (II Peter 3:13), a holy city in which there " shall no more be anything accursed, but the throne of God and of the Lamb shall be in it, and his servants shall worship him . . ." (Rev. 22:3).

CHAPTER VIII | *Christian Marriage*

There is scarcely anything about which Catholics are more aware of differences with Protestants than Christian marriage. They continually meet these difficulties in connection with practical questions like these: Who should perform marriage services? Ought Catholics to marry Protestants? Why do Protestants allow divorces? What about birth control? To such questions Catholics have their own answers, and they usually know that Protestants have different answers.

Protestants, for their part, would urge Catholics to believe that Protestants are as interested as Catholics in upholding Christian marriage. It is not enough for Protestants to be concerned about marriage for ordinary men. They must be concerned about marriage as God would have marriage for Christians — which is to say that they must be concerned about Christian marriage.

The Protestant understanding of Christianity that expresses this concern will be described in three parts. The first part deals with Christian marriage in a general way. The other two parts deal with special matters in connection with divorce and childbirth.

I

First then, Christian marriage.

What makes a marriage to be a Christian marriage? To begin with, here is the general Protestant answer: a marriage is Christian when a husband and wife who are children of God seek to make their marriage what God, through the Bible, wants it to be.

Protestants, then, differ from Catholics over what Catholics hold to be the sacramental nature of marriage. For Catholics, there is marriage between unbaptized persons — natural or non-Christian marriage — which is quite a proper type of marriage. But Christian marriage is a sacrament. Hence, when two baptized persons are married, whether they are both Catholics or Protestants, their marriage is a Christian marriage if they enter into it as a sacrament. To do so, they must intend their marriage to be a sacrament, and they must obey the laws the Catholic Church sets up to govern it, unless the church chooses to grant them exceptions. Although they themselves are the ministers or agents of their marriage, they must contract it along with the blessing of a priest. As a sacrament, their marriage becomes a divine bond uniting them for life. Moreover it brings them sanctifying grace; and sanctifying grace imparts to them that supernatural life by which they can live within marriage as they ought to live, that is, in a relationship with each other similar to that between Christ and his church described in Eph. 5:24-25: "As the church is subject to Christ, so let wives be subject in everything to their husbands. Husbands, love your wives, as Christ loved the church and gave himself up for her." If Catholics do not so contract marriage as a sacrament, they are not truly married. Moreover, they are guilty of mortal sin, the sin that damns eternally.

Protestants, however, do not believe that a marriage between Christians becomes Christian through becoming a sacrament. In their view, Christian marriage is not a sacrament. Even some Catholic scholars, they observe, grant that if the Catholic Church did not authoritatively declare Christian marriage to be a sacrament, they would have difficulty in finding evidence for its sacramental nature either in the Bible or in apostolic tradition. In rejecting the sacramental nature of Christian marriage, Protestants also reject the Catholic claim to have exclusive control over the marriage of baptized persons. Furthermore, they reject the idea that through sanctifying grace Christians are given the ability to make their lives within Christian marriage what they ought to be. To them, once more, the relationship suggested between men and God is too mechanical, too impersonal; and it tends, therefore, to make difficult its announced purpose.

Protestants believe that a marriage becomes Christian as any social relationship among men becomes Christian — only as the people in it seek constantly to follow the will of God as he speaks through the Bible. Friendship becomes Christian when friends try to be the kind of friends the God of the Bible wants them to be; governments become Christian when citizens try to be the kind of citizens God wants them to be. Similarly, marriage becomes Christian when husbands and wives try to be the kind of husbands and wives God wants them to be. In their essence, or in their being, marriages between Christians and non-Christians are the same. They are both common as all things of the world are common — both are the creation of the God of history — and so on that score neither is any better than the other. But marriage between Christians becomes uncommon as all things of the world become uncommon — when the sons of God submit themselves to the will of their Father who is the God of history, in order that his will may be done with them and through them. Marriage becomes Christian, therefore, when husbands and wives recognize a continuing personal encounter with God.

For Protestants, it follows from the observation of the two preceding paragraphs that churches have only teaching authority over the marriage of Christians, not administrative authority. Christians living together as churches should help one another to know God's will. Hence churches should teach their young people what Christian marriage is, and help the husbands and wives among them to live in Christian marriage. In fact, as a witness to their convictions, churches may sometimes refuse to marry persons whom they believe have no intention or prospect of living in Christian marriage. But churches can do this only as a witness, as a means by which they teach the nature of Christian marriage. If the persons whom they refuse to marry insist on being married, the churches have no right to prevent them from being married in some other way. And to say that the churches have no such right is also to say this: if the persons insist on being married in some other way, then the churches have no authority to declare them sinners. That only God can do.

For Protestants, it also follows from the observations of the paragraphs above that civil marriages between Christians are valid. Marriage between Christians is common as all things of the world are common; so the marriage contract can be validated — made official — as other contracts are validated, by the state. In fact, a marriage ceremony performed by a clerygman is valid because the clergyman represents not only his church; he also represents the state as one given authority by the state to validate the marriage contract; Christians, it seems to Protestants, can object to civil marriages only when such marriages require them to affirm or do something contrary to what is proper for Christians. Otherwise, civil ceremonies marry individuals just as truly as church ceremonies do, but have nothing to do with whether their marriages are Christian or unchristian. Whether their marriages are Christian or unchristian depends upon what they make of them. It depends, that is, on whether or not they try to live within their marriages as the husbands and wives the God of the Bible wants them to be.

But, Protestants believe, just because Christian marriage is what it is, it is fitting and desirable that Christians should be married in church ceremonies. In such ceremonies they formally announce before the church, the Christian community, that they intend to make their marriages Christian. This announcement strengthens their intention. And in return the church promises to help them fulfill it. At the same time, both those being married, and the church through the officiating clergymen, pray God's blessing upon the marriages. Accordingly, most dedicated Protestants are married by their pastors in church ceremonies held either in the church buildings or in their homes. In addition, some Protestant denominations provide for those who wish them church ceremonies to bless civil marriages. The ceremonies do not marry, or in any sense remarry the couple; in the Protestant view they are already fully married. The ceremonies simply help them experience the same spiritual strengthening known by couples in church ceremonies.

But what, specifically, makes the marriage of two Christians a Christian marriage? Just how, that is, does God want them to live to make their marriage a Christian marriage?

To begin with, God wants of them exactly what he wants of non-Christians who are married. First, God wants them to live as husband and wife for all their life. Secondly, God wants them to minister to the needs of each other — each other's religious, social, and physical needs, including each other's sexual needs in a monogamous fashion. Thirdly, God wants them to have children, and to provide for their children's physical and educational requirements.

It should be observed that Protestants, unlike Catholics, believe that God makes the service of husband and wife to each other more important in marriage than the having and training of children. They should have children if they can. But the second chapter of Genesis says that God decided to give Adam a wife simply because he was lonely;

and Jesus, speaking of marriage, mentioned only one purpose for it, that husband and wife should be one. A husband and wife should minister to each other's needs before they have children, while they have children, after the children have grown up and left them, and when, unfortunately, they can have no children.

But if, to begin with, God wants of Christian husbands and wives exactly what he wants of non-Christian husbands and wives, what more does he require of the partners in a Christian marriage? He wants them to carry out his basic desires for all marriage according to his special will as he makes it known through Jesus Christ. But what, specifically, does that mean?

Through Christ, God shows that he wants Christian husbands and wives to suffer crucifixion, if necessary, to keep their marriage a lifelong one. Christ continued to obey God although his obedience took him to the cross; and Christian husbands and wives should continue to obey God's will that their marriage should be lifelong even though their obedience takes them to the cross. Here the language is illustrative, of course. But the meaning is clear: Christian husbands and wives should be willing to pay any personal price to preserve their marriages until death alone separates them.

Through Christ, God shows that he wants Christian husbands and wives to minister to each other through selfless love. Christ ministered to men's needs, seeking nothing for himself; and Christian husbands and wives should minister to each other's needs, seeking nothing for themselves — not even happiness. This is selfless love which alone is true love. And, it should be added, a husband who so loves does not expect his wife to obey him, nor does a wife expect to obey her husband. They simply love; and that is enough to inspire them constantly to seek each other's good. So it is that in Protestant marriage ceremonies brides are scarcely ever asked to promise to obey husbands. That is an old formula which a deeper understanding of love as it appears in Christ makes outmoded. So usually Protestant brides take the same vow their grooms take, something like "to love, honor, and cherish."

Through Christ, God shows that he wants Christian husbands and wives to bring up their children "in the discipline and instruction of the Lord" (Eph. 6:4) . Christ came to call men to salvation through the God of the Bible, and Christian parents should call their children to that salvation. They are responsible, therefore, for doing everything they can to train their children in the knowledge and experience of God.

But in the light of this entire Protestant position about marriage and Christians, what do Protestants believe about mixed marriages, marriages of Protestants with Catholics? Protestants believe that all mixed marriages are valid so long as they are approved by the state, whether they are performed by an officer of the state, or by a Protestant or Catholic clergyman with the approval of the state. Furthermore, Protestants believe that mixed marriages can be Christian if the husbands and wives, despite their differences, purpose to make them so. Still, Protestants encourage Protestants to marry Protestants and discourage them from marrying Catholics. Believing as they do, Protestants cannot approve the fact that the Catholic Church recognizes only mixed marriages performed by the Catholic Church subject to Catholic law, and in doing so insists that any children of the unions must be raised as Catholics. To Protestants, this contradicts the nature of marriage, and takes away the freedom given Christians by the God of the Bible. In the Protestant view, the marriages of Protestants with Protestants better serve the harmonious development of Christian faith and life, both inside and outside marriage.

Finally, Protestants would say this about Christian marriage: Christian marriage is in no way inferior to Christian celibacy. To be sure, God sometimes calls certain persons to remain unmarried. But this is not because the unmarried state is any better than the married state. It is simply because for some reason God lays upon them a special obligation. Both unmarried Christians and married Christians are equally obligated before God in the state to which he has called them — and equally honored.

II

Secondly, divorce and Christian marriage. The question here relates only to those who would make their marriage Christian. It does not concern divorce and non-Christians.

Protestants grant the possibility of divorce for Christians. In their view, under certain circumstances, divorce is justified for Christians who have sought to make their marriage Christian. Catholics, of course, altogether reject the possibility of divorce. Protestants have great respect for the Catholic view. They readily understand how it is an effort on the part of Catholics to further what Protestants also believe to be the will of God, lifelong marriage. On the other hand, they observe that in the opinion of some Catholic scholars divorce on the ground of adultery was approved by certain early Catholic synods. And they believe themselves to have good reason for thinking that sometimes divorce for Christians is not only permissible but necessary.

Still, Protestants discourage divorce for Christians. Their ministers counsel with brides and grooms to prepare them for lifelong marriage, and advise those in marriage difficulties against divorce save as a last resort. Protestants oppose laws that encourage divorce by making it easy. They are reluctant to approve the remarriage of divorced persons without qualifications. For example, some denominations remarry only the innocent party (innocent so-called) of a divorce, while one denomination requires both parties to wait normally for at least a year before remarriage, and then remarries them after they repent of their past failure in marriage and firmly vow to succeed this time. These Protestant efforts to discourage divorce are very largely successful. There are few divorces among dedicated Protestants.

Here it may be added, somewhat incidentally, that in at least one respect Protestants are stricter with regard to what can be called the morality of bringing a marriage relationship to an end. Though the Catholic Church does not grant divorces, it does grant annulments for marriages that in its judgment are invalid. It does not, however, necessarily require the partners of an invalid marriage to separate immediately unless their continued relationship should become publicly known and scandalous. Protestants, however, call upon the partners of an invalid marriage, even though they alone know their marriage to be invalid, to separate immediately.

On the other hand, in holding divorces to be occasionally permissible and necessary, Protestants think along some lines similar to those taken by the Catholic Church in justifying annulments. The Catholic Church annuls a marriage entered into by Catholics contrary to its laws even though the parties may have lived together for years and had children. By its action the Catholic Church recognizes that, through disobeying its laws, the parties have created a situation in which their formal marriage has no meaning. No real marriage exists. At the same time, by its action the Catholic Church recognizes that the continuance of the formal marriage can only lead the parties into further sin. Since no real marriage exists, for the parties to continue living together in a formal marriage is immoral.

Similarly, Protestants believe that a divorce is justified when real marriages between Christians have ceased to exist without reasonable prospect of renewal. A Christian husband and wife live in Christian marriage when they are faithful to God, and therefore faithful to each other, by making their marriage what God wants it to be. But suppose they become faithless to God and to each other. Suppose they express their faithlessness in one of several ways, in desertion, sexual infidelity, nonsupport, or in abuse, psychological, physical, or spiritual, of the other spouse or their children. Then they destroy their marriage as a real marriage: it becomes dead. In this situation, to require them to live together in formal marriage is to require them to live a lie—as though they were married when they are not married. It is to require them to live immorally — in a sort of legalized prostitution. And it is to require their children to live under conditions that harm rather than help them. In this situation, just as for Catholics an annulment is a public and formal recognition that no marriage exists, so for Protestants a divorce is a public and formal recognition that marriage has ceased to exist.

Protestants think that their position on divorce does not differ from what Jesus taught. In their judgment, Christ never made Christian marriage a sacrament; so marriage is not an unbreakable union. Moreover, when Jesus spoke against divorce, he was not speaking against the Protestant opinion of today; he was speaking against the Jewish opinion of his day, based on the Mosaic law, that husbands could divorce their wives whenever they pleased. In fact, Protestants think, Jesus left the door open, not only for divorce on the ground of adultery, but for divorce on other grounds. In Matt., ch. 19, he granted the possibility of divorce on the ground of adultery. And, as was observed in the last chapter, Jesus held that God's laws should be interpreted, not legalistically, but in the light of the circumstances. To Protestants it seems proper, therefore, to interpret Jesus' own sayings nonlegalistically. If that is done, then acts of desertion, nonsupport, and persistent abuse are forms of adultery. For adultery, in essence, is simply a sign of faithlessness to God and one's spouse, and these other acts are signs also of that faithlessness.

Protestants, like Catholics, admit that the sayings of Jesus are difficult to interpret. Jesus can be quoted both for divorce (Matt. 5:32; 19:9) and against it (Mark 10:10-12; Luke 16:18). But Protestants, unlike Catholics, resort to no infallible magisterium of the church for an infallible and authoritative answer. They admit the difficulty of interpreting Jesus' statements, continue to admit it, and persist in trying to determine just what they mean.

But Protestants are encouraged in thinking that their understanding of Jesus' view on divorce is correct by their observation of one of Jesus' clearest characteristics, his opposition to pretense. Jesus wanted men to speak and act as they are, not as they are not, which is why he so sternly rebuked hypocrisy. But for Christian husbands and wives to remain formally married when they are no longer really married is to act out what is not — to live a lie. Divorce, however, is honest. It shows what is a fact — that they are no longer really married. And because divorce is honest, Protestants believe, it agrees with Jesus' desire for honesty instead of pretense.

III

Thirdly, childbirth. Here the Protestant attitude on two matters connected with childbirth will be discussed — birth control, and the medical treatment of wives whose lives are endangered by the bearing of children.

In their own ways, both Protestants and Catholics approve of birth control. Protestants approve any ordinary method of birth control, including the use of drugs and mechanical devices. Catholics approve only the rhythm method, which avoids conception by limiting intercourse to those days between menstrual periods when women are unlikely to conceive. To speak more accurately, the Catholic Church approves only the rhythm method. Birth control is considered a matter of Christian morals over which Catholics must accept the authority of their church. Protestants, however, are individually responsible for their own decisions, although their churches may give them advice.

The Catholic Church approves the rhythm method of birth control because, for one thing, it says that the rhythm method is natural. The rhythm method conforms to established laws of nature, making use of the free periods for intercourse provided by nature. Drugs or mechanical devices, on the other hand, work against the established laws of nature. They prevent conception when nature makes conception possible.

Protestants, for their part, believe that birth control by drugs or mechanical devices is equally natural. The God of history has made men subject to the laws of nature, and yet superior to them. He enables them to modify or check the operation of some laws of nature by using other laws. A small boy, for example, so checks the operations of the law of gravity whenever he catches a ball. And because God has so provided, it is just as natural for men to modify or check the operations of the laws of nature as it is for them to conform to those laws. Hence, it is not unnatural for men to use drugs or mechanical devices to check the operation of the law of conception. The only question is whether it is right for them to practice birth control at all. But if it is, then it is as right for them to use drugs and mechanical means as it is for them to use the rhythm method.

The Catholic Church approves the rhythm method of birth control because, in the second place, it says, the rhythm method disciplines sex desire to its chief purpose — the propagation of the race. But when men use drugs or mechanical devices to prevent conception, they cause sex desire to serve physical gratification primarily, for then they can satisfy it whenever they please without fear of having children. When men use the rhythm method of birth control, however, they are constantly reminded that the primary purpose of sex is propagation.

Protestants, for their part, approve other methods of birth control because they believe that the primary purpose of sex desire in men is to express love. The primary purpose of sex in animals is propagation, but the primary purpose of sex in men is to express the love husbands and wives have for each other. Certainly this is the purpose of sex if husbands and wives are living as Christians in love for each other. Of course, if they are living as animals do, or simply to gratify their own selfish impulse, that is another matter. To be sure, husbands and wives must never forget that through sex they are responsible under God for having children. But, if birth control itself is right, then it is proper for them to use means that allow them freedom at any time to express their love for each other through the sex experience.

Furthermore, there is the question of the medical treatment of wives whose lives are endangered by the bearing of children. Here the first interest of Protestants is to protect the wives even if it requires the loss of children or the ability to conceive. Accordingly, if a pregnancy seriously threatens the health or life of a mother, Protestants approve a therapeutic abortion. Or if during childbirth the lives of both mother and child are in danger, Protestants approve the saving of the mother even though the child is lost. Or if a possible pregnancy or childbirth would probably cause permanent injury or death, Protestants approve the sterilizing of the wife or the husband.

Catholics, however, disapprove such action as being forms of murder or refusals to endure suffering. Catholics would solve the problems mentioned by continence, or abstinence from sex relations, so that there would be no pregnancies. Like the use of the rhythm method of birth control, continence, Catholics believe, is a natural solution. It is a natural solution because it operates without destroying nature, as do such methods as therapeutic abortion, the loss of child at birth to save the mother, and sterilization.

Protestants, on the other hand, do not believe that the fetus, whether it is nine days or nine months old, is yet a person who can be murdered. Moreover, they think that if sterilization is murder because it prevents the conception of children, then continence, because it does the same thing, is also murder. In addition, they see nothing wrong in the avoidance of unnecessary suffering. Christ himself would have avoided the cross if he could. Also, to them prolonged continence in marriage prevents both the normal expression of love through sex and the satisfaction of normal sexual needs.

Finally, in the judgment of Protestants, there are the social responsibilities of wives to be considered. When wives cannot fulfill their obligation to have children without serious harm to themselves, then they have a greater obligation. It is the obligation to fulfill their responsibilities to their husbands, their families, and society. It is their greater obligation to life already existent, whereas their obligation to bear children is their lesser obligation to life as yet only potential.

CHAPTER IX | *Education*

In the United States there are the public schools and alongside the public schools the Catholic parochial schools. Both are the most extensive and the most highly developed schools of their types in the world. The public schools are set up and maintained by the state to provide the children of the United States with a general and non-sectarian education. The Catholic parochial schools are set up and maintained by the Catholic Church to provide the Catholic children of the United States, and any others who wish to enroll, with a general and Catholic education.

In recent years American Protestants and Catholics have often found themselves disagreeing over these public and parochial schools. Protestants, with some exceptions as will be seen, support the public schools. Catholics support their parochial schools. Besides, Catholics seek for their parochial schools, and in some instances have secured for them, tax-provided services like textbooks, school lunches, and school bus transportation. Moreover, Catholics hold that their parochial schools ought to be given a share of the regular school taxes. Protestants, again with some exceptions, think otherwise on these points. The results have been, and continue to be, court suits involving Catholics and Protestants, rival Catholic and Protestant maneuvering behind the scenes in both state and national politics, and political, business, and social conflicts among Catholics and Protestants living in the same communities.

The Catholic and Protestant debate over the parochial

or public-school issue shows no signs of declining. Rather, it is intensifying, and probably will continue to intensify for a long time. On the one hand, American Catholics are expanding their parochial schools. As they do so, they are becoming more and more concerned to obtain help for their schools from tax-supported community services and from tax funds themselves. On the other hand, most American Protestants are emphasizing the importance of public schools. As they do so, they are becoming more and more concerned that taxes be used, indirectly through tax-supported public services and directly through actual grants, only for the public schools. Hence it is that the issue of parochial or public schools will be increasingly debated by Catholics and Protestants.

Clearly, the parochial or public-school issue is a very practical matter about which American Catholics and Protestants need carefully to explain their respective viewpoints to each other. Catholics must explain to Protestants, and Protestants must explain to Catholics, why they think as they do. Consequently here, in behalf of the Protestants, an explanation is attempted. The explanation proceeds by describing first the general Protestant approach to the problem; then it goes on to present the reasons why most American Protestants support public schools.

I

To begin with, the general Protestant approach to the problem of parochial or public schools.

It has already been indicated that not all Protestants regard the parochial- or public-school issue in the same way. Although most American Protestants favor public schools, not all do. For example, one of the larger American Protestant denominations, the Missouri Synod Lutheran, maintains its own parochial schools at the grammar school level; and individual Christian day schools, supported by local groups of Protestants, are not uncommon. Moreover, although American Protestants do not favor tax assistance for parochial schools, Protestants outside the United States often do. Thus, in Quebec and the Netherlands, Protestants generally approve of the allocation of tax funds to both Catholic and Protestant schools. In addition, American Protestants who support public schools inside the United States sometimes set up parochial schools both inside and outside the United States. Thus they maintain mission schools in the United States for Indians, and in Africa for the native peoples.

Such diversity of practice and opinion among Protestants relative to parochial and public schools develops from several convictions held by Protestants generally. These convictions are four; and they divide into two pairs. The first pair has to do with Christians and education as a whole. The second pair has to do with the state from which tax benefits for parochial schools must come.

There are then the two convictions held by Protestants about Christians and education as a whole:

1. All Christians are responsible for the education of children. The Heavenly Father cares for his earthly children's needs, and parents are to care for their children's needs, which include education. They are to bring up their children " in the discipline and instruction of the Lord " (Eph. 6:4) , and to see that they receive broad training for life. But Christians as a group also share that responsibility. As those bound to join with Christ in concern for all men's needs, they must be attentive to children's educational needs.

2. God does not indicate exactly how Christians should meet their responsibility for the education of children. In the Protestant view, the Bible gives neither their churches nor the Catholic Church final authority over education. Nor does the Bible specify that Christians should set up schools. In fact, the Bible nowhere gives detailed

instructions about how Christians should go about educating children.

Then there are the two convictions held by Protestants about the state:

1. The state is responsible for serving God as he is revealed in Jesus Christ. Through Christ, God is pre-eminent over all things " in heaven and on earth, visible and invisible, whether thrones or dominions or principalities or authorities " (Col. 1:16). Christ is ruler over nature and men. He is ruler over the state. And the state, therefore, is responsible for seeking his will and doing it.

2. God does not indicate how the state is to serve God where the education of children is concerned. As Protestants see it, the Bible gives neither their churches nor the Catholic Church authority to tell the state what its educational policy should be. Nor does the Bible indicate what the state's educational policy should be. In fact, the Bible nowhere gives detailed instructions about how the state should go about educating children.

From each of these pairs of convictions Protestants draw a conclusion. From the first pair they draw this conclusion: God leaves Christians free to work out methods for educating children. Although God makes Christians responsible for the education of children, he leaves them free to work out educational projects and procedures. From the second pair Protestants draw this conclusion: God leaves Christians free to ask specific educational policies from the state. Although God makes the state responsible for serving him, he leaves Christians free to decide what, if any, educational responsibility the state should have.

These two conclusions lead Protestants on to their general position about parochial and public schools. In their view, God does not say exactly how they are to meet the educational responsibility he lays upon them; so Protestants are neither for nor against parochial or public schools as such. Furthermore, in their view, God does not say exactly what the state must do for education within its obligation to serve him; so Protestants are neither for nor against state tax assistance of parochial schools as such. Consequently, Protestants do not believe themselves required by God always to favor or to oppose parochial or public schools, or always to favor or to oppose tax assistance of parochial schools. God leaves them free to decide, in any given place or time, one way or the other.

The Catholic position is both similar and dissimilar to the Protestant position on parochial and public schools. Catholics, like Protestants, find no detailed instruction in the Bible for or against parochial or public schools. Consequently, Catholics sometimes favor parochial schools and sometimes favor public schools. But Catholics, unlike Protestants, do not do so because they think themselves left free by God to decide; they do so because they accept the decision of the Catholic Church. For Catholics the Catholic Church, through its infallible magisterium, has final authority to direct the education of children.

The Catholic position is also both similar and dissimilar to the Protestant position on tax support of parochial schools. Catholics, like Protestants, find no detailed instructions in the Bible about the state's duties in education. Consequently, Catholics sometimes favor and sometimes disfavor tax benefits for parochial schools. But again, in doing so, Catholics act with reasons different from those of Protestants. They act not because they believe themselves free before God to act, but because they accept the decisions of the Catholic Church. For Catholics the Catholic Church, through its infallible magisterium, has final authority to decide whether or not state funds should be used for parochial schools.

As Protestants undertake to meet their educational responsibilities they agree with Catholics on the need for schools of some type. Christian parents and individuals lack the knowledge and time, and sometimes the interest, to teach children everything they need to know. Schools, therefore, are necessary. But what kind of schools? Parochial schools? Public schools? And how should they be supported? As has been observed, Protestants give different answers depending upon the circumstances.

In all circumstances Protestants favor the establishment of specialized church schools supported by the churches. Protestants believe themselves responsible for teaching children to be Christians, and they would meet that responsibility through specialized church schools. These are schools like Sunday church schools, confirmation or church membership classes, summer camps, and conferences. These schools do not, like parochial schools, teach general subjects such as the three R's — reading, writing, and arithmetic. Instead, they teach particular Christian subjects such as Bible and church history, and Christian beliefs, missions, and ethics.

But sometimes Protestants favor Protestant parochial schools. This is the case when they think circumstances require parochial schools if they are to teach children Christianity effectively as they see it. For example, Protestants set up parochial schools when the public schools are so anti-Christian that they may influence children away from Christianity. Or, for example, Protestants set up parochial schools when the only schools available are Catholic schools which may influence children away from the Protestant conception of Christianity.

The concern that Protestants sometimes have for Protestant parochial schools helps them sympathize with Catholics in their concern for Catholic parochial schools. Protestants so much believe in their conception of Christianity that to teach it to children they will, if necessary, set up Protestant parochial schools. Hence, Protestants can understand how Catholics, fervently believing in their conception of Christianity, can organize Catholic parochial schools. In fact, Protestants so much respect the Catholic position that they defend the privilege of Catholics to have parochial schools.

As for tax benefits for parochial schools, Protestants sometimes approve of them. There are times when the citizenry wish to aid the religious teaching of the parochial schools. There are also times when the citizenry wish to aid the general teaching of the parochial schools, the teaching of the three R's and the like. In such circumstances, Protestants sometimes think, tax benefits can properly be given to parochial schools as an expression of the will of the people provided two conditions are met: that the parochial schools are left free to teach religion as they see fit; and that all parochial schools — of whatever religion — are offered equal tax benefits.

On the other hand, there are cases when Protestants support public schools and oppose tax benefits for parochial schools. The situation in the United States belongs, of course, to the latter cases. In the United States, as everywhere, Protestants seek to fulfill their educational responsibility under God in the light of the circumstances. Most of them favor public schools as the only schools to be supported by taxes. Why they do so the next section of the chapter goes on to explain.

II

Over 90 per cent of today's American Protestants favor public schools. Prior to around 1840, no public schools existed in the United States, and American Protestants supported a variety of parochial and private schools that taught both Christian and general subjects. After 1840, however, public schools began to develop rapidly. In the next sixty years practically every state adopted constitutional provisions prohibiting the use of tax funds for either parochial or private schools. For a time there was a considerable Protestant opposition to the public-school movement, but this quickly declined except among a small minority. Today, America's Protestants are overwhelmingly for the public schools and against the allocation of state funds to any other kind of school.

In favoring public schools, however, Protestants also recognize the need of specialized church schools of their own. These specialized church schools can be called, more broadly speaking, the educational activities of the Protestant Church. They include educational projects such as vacation church schools, summer conferences, children's choirs, young people's societies, even nursery schools. Especially they include the Sunday church schools. Local Protestant churches provide leaders and teachers, usually voluntary, for their educational activities, and often construct costly educational buildings. Protestant denominations, separately and together, do extensive teacher training and prepare study materials. And Protestant local churches and denominations constantly urge parents to support their educational activities through their gifts, and through seeing to it that their children attend them.

American Protestants maintain their own specialized church schools for a profoundly Christian reason: they would have their children know and grow in the knowl edge of Jesus Christ as their Lord. Christians are responsible for urging all men to accept Jesus Christ as Lord; and they must begin with the children. American Protestants do this through their specialized church schools. Through these schools they would bring their children to accept the Christian faith as they understand it.

At the same time, American Protestants make two observations that lead them also to support public schools. The first observation is related to the religious pluralism of America. The second observation is related to the general perception of truth.

The American community is pluralistic in its religious character. It includes, that is, adherents of numerous religions: Roman, Orthodox, and Eastern Catholics; Protestants of many denominations; Jews of several types; representatives in lesser numbers of the world's great religions. All these live together in the same nation. America is not a community of one religious faith; it is a community of many religious faiths.

Amidst the religious pluralism of America it is necessary for people of various religious faiths to live together in mutual understanding and appreciation. It is necessary if what now seems to be the will of God is to be maintained: this is American democracy. In America the people join together to govern; hence, they must know and respect one another. Moreover, quite apart from the existence of American democracy it is always the will of God that people of all religious faiths should live together in justice and good will as sons of the same God. And of that Christians, who know the love of God expressed through Jesus Christ, should be most aware.

It is the observation of American Protestants that the American public schools make a unique contribution toward teaching children to live in understanding and appreciation of one another. Other American schools contribute much to that objective, Catholic and Protestant parochial schools as well as specialized Protestant church schools. But the public schools do it in a way peculiar to them and of special importance. Whereas for the most part other schools bring together children of one religion, the public schools bring together children of all America's religions, Catholic, Protestant, Jewish, and the rest. And thereby the public schools provide one of the most important means for teaching children of different religions to grow in regard for one another. Parochial and specialized church schools, for their part, teach children of particular religious faiths to respect children of other religious faiths by telling them to do so. Public schools, however, teach children of particular religious faiths to respect children of other religious faiths by causing them to live together. In the public schools, Protestant, Catholic, Jewish, and other children study, work, and play together, and so come to understand and appreciate one another.

Then there is the second observation made by American Protestants in their support of American public schools, the observation related to the perception of truth.

The perception of truth that God offers to men — the truth of religion, and science, and art, and politics, and all truth — is benefited by the religiously neutral approach to truth. This approach tries to examine truth apart from religious assumptions or convictions. When men take this approach to truth, they often see things not seen before. Religious assumptions or convictions, whether Catholic, Protestant, Jewish, or otherwise, can close up men's minds to facts as they really are. This happens, for example, when Catholics and Protestants, convinced that God created all things, refuse to admit what science shows to have occurred, that the world and its life appeared in some sort of evolutionary fashion. On the other hand, the religiously neutral approach to truth can open men's minds to whatever the truth may be, and encourage men to recognize and admit it.

It is the observation of American Protestants that the American public schools take the religiously neutral attitude, and thereby benefit their students' perception of truth. The public schools adopt no religious viewpoint, Catholic, Protestant, Jewish, or otherwise; religiously neutral, they seek to present knowledge to their students apart from religious convictions. This often enables them to bring out truth that parochial and specialized church schools, because of their religiously biased approach to truth, easily ignore or distort. There is, for example, the history of the so-called European wars of religion, wars in the sixteenth and seventeenth centuries when Catholics and Protestants fought each other. It is easy for Catholic parochial schools, with Catholic convictions, to teach that these were simply wars in which devoted Catholics battled heroically for their faith against Protestants; and it is just as easy for Protestant specialized church schools, with Protestant convictions, to teach that these were simply wars in which devoted Protestants battled heroically for their faith against Catholics. But the public schools, religiously neutral, are much more inclined to teach that those who fought on both sides of the wars of religion were as often as not prompted by greed, hate, and lust for power. So it is throughout the whole field of knowledge. The public schools, because they are religiously neutral, contribute greatly to showing children the facts as they are.

On the basis of these two observations, American Protestants support the American public schools. As they see it, without the public schools, children would not learn nearly so well what they need to learn and what the public schools do so much to help teach them. They would not learn to understand and appreciate Americans who hold other religions, nor would they learn nearly so well to perceive the truth objectively. In fact, American Protestants believe, in these connections, that the American public schools serve so well that there is no substitute for them. America cannot do without its public schools. And so American Protestants support them.

At the same time, however, American Protestants willingly accept the existence of parochial schools for Catholics and for other religious groups. Regarding public schools so highly, they wish that there were only public schools, but they are willing, with two provisos, to allow parochial schools because they respect the rights of parents to determine what schools their children should attend. The one proviso is: the parochial schools should carry on adequate programs of general studies, the three R's and the rest. The other proviso is: the parochial schools should teach their students how to co-operate with the people of

America's other religions in the maintenance of American democracy. So long as parochial schools meet these conditions, Protestants believe, parents can properly send their children to them. For this is their right as parents with authority over the education of their children, and this is their right as religious persons bound to do their duty before God as they see it.

Still, Protestants are unwilling for parochial schools to receive tax benefits for strictly instructional purposes. Some are willing for the students of parochial schools to receive tax-provided social services such as medical examinations and surplus food for school lunches, and some are even willing to include bus transportation. But almost all Protestants oppose the assignment of tax funds to parochial schools to be used for direct school expenses such as the construction and maintenance of buildings and the payment of teachers' salaries. To do this would seriously harm the public schools. It would deprive them of needed income. It would make the public schools appear to have no special significance. And eventually it would limit the work of the public schools by encouraging the development of parochial schools.

There are further reasons why American Protestants believe that only public schools should receive tax funds. On the one hand, they accept the constitutionally established American principle of the separation of church and state. As was pointed out earlier, Protestants believe that the Bible allows Christians freedom to develop relations between church and state which are, in given situations, most agreeable with Christian faith and life. And in America, Protestants believe, these relations involve the separation of church and state. On the other hand, the separation of church and state requires the state to be neutral toward religion — it must advocate no religion. Hence it is improper for American state funds to be used to support parochial schools that, as parochial schools, advocate particular religions. State funds can properly be used for the general advantage of all religions. And they are so used when they are used to support public schools. For public schools offer the children of all religions equal religious opportunities without favoring any particular religion.

But is the refusal of tax funds to parochial schools unjust? Catholics think so. It is, they say, contrary to distributive justice. Since Catholics prefer their own parochial schools, and since Catholics pay school taxes, it is only right, they think, that some assignment of the taxes be made to them. At the most, all school taxes paid by Catholics should be given to their parochial schools. At the least, a substantial share of the taxes should be given.

American Protestants recognize the earnestness and sincerity with which American Catholics state their case, but just as earnestly and sincerely American Protestants think otherwise. The will of the American people is that tax funds should be used only for public schools; therefore, all tax funds may properly be used for the public schools even though Catholic taxpayers compose a dissenting minority. After all, taxes paid by all the people are often used for purposes disapproved by minorities. Moreover, Catholics are allowed to send their children to Catholic parochial schools even though the great majority of the American people believe that public schools offer highly important advantages. Thus Catholics are allowed to do what most Americans, for reasons good and sufficient to them, do not do; and it is right that Catholics should be asked to make their own financial provisions for their own parochial schools.

CHAPTER X | *History*

This final chapter takes a quick look at Protestant history. Just as Protestants can better appreciate the nature and vitality of Catholicism by knowing something of its history, so Catholics can better appreciate the nature and vitality of Protestantism by knowing something of its history. Moreover, Catholic accounts of Protestant history can easily be more accurate in some judgments than Protestant accounts: Protestant historians, favoring Protestantism are likely to miss some things that Catholic historians, not favoring Protestantism, see. On the other hand, Protestant accounts of Protestant history can easily be more accurate in some respects than Catholic accounts: Catholic historians, not favoring Protestantism, are naturally less sympathetic toward what took place than Protestant historians, favoring Protestantism. Surely, then, Catholics need to learn about Protestant history from the Protestant as well as from the Catholic viewpoint.

Since Protestantism is over four hundred years old, one brief chapter can tell its history only in a very broad way. To do so, the chapter relates events to the great historical challenges which were heard by Protestants through history and the Bible. As God regularly makes known his present will to his sons, he has confronted Protestants with situations that have sent them to their Bibles, there to hear him challenge them to action. Thus Protestant history is described as Protestants have responded to three challenges: the challenge to the reformation of the church, to the expansion of the church, and to unity in Christ.

I

First, the challenge of God's call to the reformation of the church.

The challenge to the reformation of the church was experienced by many Christians between the years 1400 and 1700. It was in response to that challenge that Protestantism began. Thus it was that thousands of European Catholics left the Catholic Church to become Protestants and to establish Protestant churches. Of course, these thousands of Protestants first experienced the challenge to the reformation of the church while they were still officially Catholics. Even then, however, the challenge belongs to their history as Protestants because they became Protestants by responding to it.

In the early sixteenth and seventeenth centuries thousands of devout European Catholics were dissatisfied with the Catholic Church. The Catholic Church was failing to meet fully their spiritual needs. In this situation they studied the Bible. Then as they looked back at the Catholic Church in the light of the Bible it seemed to them that the Catholic Church was not the church as the Bible required the church to be. The doctrines of the Catholic Church were not in full agreement with the Bible, and the life of the Catholic Church, expressed in the lives of many of its laity and its clergy, was often grossly ignorant and immoral.

At this point these thousands of European Christians saw through the Bible a historical challenge, a call from God to Christian action. The Bible declared to them what the Christian church should be in doctrine and life. But this, it seemed to them, the Catholic Church was not. They saw themselves challenged, therefore, to seek a more truly Christian church, a church in doctrine and life more fully in accord with the Bible. They were challenged by God to seek a reformed, or purified, church.

One of these European Christians was the noted German priest, monk, preacher, theologian, and teacher, Martin Luther. He had long sought salvation through the Catholic Church, and in obedience to its teachings he had done all manner of good works to gain salvation. Still, the sense of guilt for his sins, which meant his loss of salvation, lay heavy upon him. Seeking some solution, he had begun the study of the Bible. And the more he studied the Bible the more the conviction grew on him that the doctrines of the Catholic Church did not fully agree with the Bible. Also, he had seen so much moral corruption in the lives of Catholic monks and priests that when he compared them with the moral demands of the Bible he wondered whether the Catholic Church could truly express the will of God. In this situation he had felt himself more and more challenged to seek to reform, or to purify, the Catholic Church.

Finally, in a series of dramatic events between 1517 and 1521, Luther actually sought to reform the Catholic Church. In 1517, he questioned the validity of papal indulgences, the pope's promises to pray God to lessen a person's punishment in purgatory, provided the person does some stipulated good work. At the same time he questioned the moral right of the wealthy reigning pope, Leo X, to do what he was doing — to take for indulgences money from poor German peasants and use it toward the rebuilding of St. Peter's Church in Rome. In the next four years Luther questioned more and more Catholic doctrines, both in public debate and in written statements. It became increasingly clear, however, that the Catholic Church would not listen to him. At last, in 1521, it excommunicated him.

Unable to reform the Catholic Church, Luther now set himself to answer the challenge to reformation by declaring himself free from its jurisdiction. The Catholic Church, he said, had shown itself to be no true church: it had refused to amend its doctrines under questioning based upon the Bible. Consequently, Luther denied the right of the pope to excommunicate him. He was, he affirmed, subject only to the Word of God in the Bible; therefore he would preach and administer the sacraments according to that Word, and reshape the whole life of the church according to that Word.

Luther's experience profoundly influenced the thousands of European Catholics who sought a reformed church. They too despaired that the Catholic Church could be reformed. Encouraged by Luther's example, they denied the authority of the Catholic Church over them and proceeded to fashion their churches according to the Bible. They were people from all classes — merchants, scholars, farmers, workers, housewives, nobles, monks, priests, and even bishops. They came to be known as Protestants, not simply negative people who were complaining against something, but positive people who were testifying for something. What they testified for were Biblical teaching and practice. And as they incorporated this into their churches, those churches became known as Protestant. Thus their answer to the challenge of reformation was the Protestant Reformation with its Protestant churches.

Today's Protestants greatly appreciate the fact that many devout Catholics show much understanding of the Protestant Reformers. These Catholics grant that often the Reformers had a genuine concern to know and to obey God. Recently, outstanding Catholic scholars, especially in Europe, have written about Martin Luther with deep respect for his spiritual sincerity and zeal. Moreover, these Catholics grant that the Catholic Church of the sixteenth century needed to be morally reformed. They lament the dishonesty, the political conniving, the downright immorality that stained the lives, not only of Catholic priests, bishops, and monastics, but also of some Catholic popes.

But these Catholics cannot understand why the Protestant Reformers felt it necessary to declare themselves free of the Catholic Church. In the sixteenth century, they observe, the Catholic Church reformed itself. It called a special council, the Council of Trent, which met from 1545 to 1563, and that council undertook to cleanse the church of its moral corruption. Moreover, these Catholics suggest, had the Protestant Reformers remained Catholics their spiritual needs would have been met by the Catholic Church. For though the lives of the Catholic clergy were often morally corrupt, the doctrines of the Catholic clergy, the infallible doctrines of the Catholic Church, were true. Certainly, large numbers of Catholics who were dissatisfied with the moral life of the Catholic clergy found spiritual satisfaction in their doctrines.

Today's Protestants, however, cannot see how the Protestant Reformers could have acted otherwise than as they did. The Protestant Reformers were deeply concerned about the moral life of the Catholic clergy and monastics, which the Catholic Church did much to change. But the Protestant Reformers were also deeply concerned about the doctrines of the Catholic clergy and monastics, which the Catholic Church did nothing to change. In fact, the Council of Trent restated Catholic doctrines and emphasized their absolute truth. And so today's Protestants do not wonder that the Protestant Reformers found it necessary to fashion their churches along lines truer to the Bible.

The earliest Protestants met with immediate and continuing opposition. Some of the opposition was mild. Catholic friends and the Catholic Church tried to dissuade them from their faith. Some of the opposition was extreme. Protestants were ostracized by individual Catholics and excommunicated by the Catholic Church. They were persecuted in a variety of ways, and sometimes they lost their lives at the hands of Catholic rulers. Catholic opposition to them even contributed extensively to the wars of religion between Catholic and Protestant nations and provinces in the sixteenth and seventeenth centuries.

But Protestants of today must admit with regret that the Protestants of the sixteenth and seventeenth centuries also did some persecuting of their own. They persecuted Catholics, and even other Protestants. Sometimes they carried their persecution so far that they took the lives of both heroic Catholics and fellow Protestants. Belief in religious tolerance did not appear immediately among most Protestants. It developed slowly among a few, and it was not until about 1700 that it began to develop rapidly among Protestants as a whole.

In the face of the Catholic opposition Protestantism was sometimes unsuccessful, sometimes successful. Protestantism was unsuccessful in central and southern Europe, and in most of Ireland. There Catholic opposition either kept the people Catholic, or, if they had become Protestant, largely brought them back to Catholicism. For example, during the seventeenth century the powerful Protestant movement in France was reduced to weakness by severe persecution. Protestantism was successful, however, in northern Europe and in Great Britain with its united countries, England, Wales, and Scotland. There so many people became so thoroughly Protestant that Germany, Denmark, Finland, Sweden, Norway, and the Netherlands, along with Great Britain, could be called Protestant countries.

By 1700, generally speaking, Protestant response to the challenge of reformation had ended. The challenge had been to a reformed European church. It had been impossible to meet the challenge by reforming the European Catholic Church. Instead it had been necessary to reject Catholic authority and develop churches reformed according to Protestant principles. Catholic opposition had limited the success with which the reformed churches had grown. But by 1700 they were firmly established in much of Europe; and what is known to history as the Protestant Reformation had taken place.

II

Secondly, the challenge of God's call to the expansion of the church.

The challenge to expansion was experienced by Protestants between the years 1700 and 1900. It was in response to that challenge that Protestantism expanded from Europe into all quarters of the world. It spread across the United States and Canada, into Central and South America, into Africa, and on into Asia, Australia, and the islands of the Pacific. The challenge itself came as Protestants confronted, on the one hand, the migration of Protestants into the largely unpopulated areas of the world and, on the other hand, the existence of semi-Christian peoples in so many parts of the world. These two aspects of the challenge will first be discussed. Then, at the close of the section, something will be said about a third and very special aspect of the challenge.

For one thing, there was the challenge Protestants saw as they confronted the migration of Protestants into the largely underpopulated areas of the world.

Beginning in 1700, many European Protestants moved from Europe into what for Europeans were new lands, the New World of North and South America, and the continents of Africa and Australia. These areas had been discovered while the Protestant Reformation was going on in Europe, but there were few Protestants who had gone to live in them. For the most part there were only small groups of British Protestants who had settled in North America during the seventeenth century. From 1700 on, however, large numbers of Protestants from all over Europe went to make their homes in the new lands. They went for a variety of reasons, sometimes to escape poverty or to make money, sometimes to find freedom from political tyranny, sometimes to find freedom from persecution at the hands of Catholics and other Protestants.

Once settled on the edges of these lands, Protestants constituted centers of population from which they pushed out into the large, relatively unoccupied areas. What happened in the United States is an excellent example. In the eighteenth century, many British, Dutch, German, and other European Protestants came to make their homes along what is now the eastern seaboard of the United States. Then, toward the end of the eighteenth century and the nineteenth century, their Protestant descendants became pioneers who went to settle the western areas of the United States.

In these population movements Protestants saw a challenge to expand Protestantism. There was the movement of European Protestants into the new lands of the world. At the same time, as Protestants saw it, the Bible summoned them to remain faithful to Protestantism wherever they went. This meant that, as European Protestants settled the new lands of the world, they faced what was for them God's challenge to establish Protestant churches wherever they went. Also, there was the movement of the Protestant descendants of these European Protestants across the face of the world. Again, at the same time, they were summoned to help their fellow Protestants with the establishment of Protestant churches wherever they went. This meant that as Protestant pioneers built their homes out on the frontiers, Protestants back in the old centers of population faced what was for them God's challenge to help the pioneers build Protestant churches.

Protestants answered the challenge, and Protestantism expanded. European Protestants set up churches wherever they went. Consequently Protestantism expanded from Europe to areas like colonial America, newly explored

Africa, newly opened Australia. Protestants in the older churches sent out money and personnel to help pioneers build churches. Consequently Protestantism expanded in further areas like the American West. By 1800, Protestants had so completely answered the challenge that churches existed wherever European Protestants and their pioneer descendants had gone.

For another thing, there was the challenge Protestants saw as they confronted the existence of non-Christian peoples in so many parts of the world.

As Protestants went out from Europe and moved forward as pioneers, they became more and more impressed with the existence of non-Christian peoples all around them. They found non-Christian peoples like the Indians of North America, the Negroes of Africa, the aborigines of Australia. They turned their attention to non-Christian people like the Persians, the Chinese, the Malayans. These peoples held primitive religions such as animism, the worship of different spirits, or more advanced religions such as Mohammedanism, Hinduism, and Buddhism. They knew little or nothing of Christianity because Christianity had not been brought to them.

Again Protestants answered the challenge, and around 1700 the Protestant missionary movement began. Protestants went as missionaries to the American Indians, to India, to China, to Africa, and the islands of the Pacific; to animists, Mohammedans, Hindus, Confucianists, and Taoists — to all peoples of all religions in the uttermost parts of the earth. Sometimes they went solely as individuals. Sometimes they went as representatives of missionary societies organized by groups of Protestant churchmen apart from the Protestant church as such. Sometimes they went as representatives of the different denominations. And always they went from every country where Protestants were to be found.

Among these missionaries were men and women who,

Protestants believe, deserve to be numbered among the finest Christians who ever lived. It has been said, of course, that for Protestants saints are not what they are for Catholics. But if the word " saint " can be used to describe the lives of Christians dedicated far beyond the average, then Protestants would certainly number among the saints many of their heroic missionaries of the eighteenth and nineteenth centuries. Here were men and woman who wore out their lives freely and without stint in the service of Christ, and often gained the martyr's crown.

As the challenge to minister to the non-Christian peoples of the world was answered, Protestants expanded into all the world. Protestant missionary work did not end in 1900. It continues today. But by 1900 that work had carried Protestants into almost every corner of the world. Whereas once there had been only European Protestants, now there were Indian, and Asiatic, and African Protestants. What once had been only European Protestantism was now world-wide Protestantism. And whereas once there were only European Protestant churches, now there were Protestant churches on every continent and in almost every nation.

But something remains to be said about a very special challenge that Protestants confronted in the years of expansion. This is referred to as a special challenge because it is of particular concern to both Catholics and Protestants who seek greater mutual understanding. It was the challenge of Protestant expansion among Catholics.

In their years of expansion Protestants felt themselves challenged by God to expand among Catholics. They saw countries in the world where there were Catholics in greater or lesser numbers along with many who were pagan or semipagan, in countries such as the islands of the Philippines. They saw other countries where there were many Catholics and few Protestants, countries such as the nation of Portugal. At the same time they were true sons of the

Protestant Reformation. The Protestants of the Reformation had believed themselves challenged by God to establish Protestantism in the midst of Catholicism.

The Protestants of the years of Protestant expansion believed themselves similarly challenged, and so considered themselves bound to establish Protestantism everywhere that Catholicism existed. In part, this was because in many areas where Catholicism existed it was of a type deplored not only by Protestants but by the best Catholics. In part, also, this was because in every area where Catholicism existed it continued to maintain doctrines which, to Protestants, were not in full agreement with the Bible. Consequently, in the nineteenth century and in the years following, Protestants sent out missionaries to work in Catholic countries and among Catholics. American Protestants were especially active in sending out missionaries to Central and South America.

On the whole, Protestants do not now feel the challenge to expand Protestantism among Catholics so acutely as they did two or three generations ago. Protestants have steadily grown in appreciation of the faithfulness with which Catholics can serve the Lord Christ despite doctrines that, to Protestants, so inadequately interpret the Bible. Yet Protestants still feel the challenge to expansion among Catholics with sufficient acuteness to continue Protestant missions in Catholic countries and amidst Catholics. American Protestants, for instance, continue to send missionaries to Central and South America, and even into Italy.

Catholics, of course, look with dismay upon Protestant missionary work among them both in the past and at the present. At the worst, it seems to Catholics, such Protestant missionary work is a rejection of the true church and thereby a rejection of God's will. At the least, it seems to Catholics, such missionary work is an unbrotherly act by one group of professing Christians toward another that creates discord between them. Hence Catholics never hesitate to manifest their opposition to Protestant missions among them, whether in the past or in the present.

Nevertheless, Protestants would suggest this to Catholics: perhaps Catholics, without abandoning their opposition to Protestant missions among them, can come to understand and even to respect Protestants in carrying on that work. Catholics, on their side, conduct missions among Protestants. For example, there is a Catholic mission to Protestants in the State of North Carolina, where the population is predominantly Protestant. Also, for several years the Knights of Columbus, through advertisements in the public press, have sought the conversion of Protestants, among others, to Catholicism. Perhaps Catholics can come to understand and even to respect Protestants in conducting missions among Catholics if they recognize that both of them are moved to missionary activity in the other group by similar impulses. Catholics are moved to their missionary activity because they are convinced of the truth of their position, and because in obedience to God and in love for their fellow men they would have everyone know it. And Protestants are likewise moved to their missionary activity. They too are convinced of the truth of their position, and they too in obedience to God and in love for their fellow men would have everyone know it. Perhaps, therefore, Catholics can come to understand and respect in Protestants what exists in themselves.

III

Thirdly, the challenge of God's call to unity in Christ.

From its beginning, Protestantism has been persistently characterized by division into numerous denominations. Protestant denominations existed in the first Protestant century, the sixteenth, and in succeeding centuries new denominations appeared. Basically, the reason was the freedom Protestants experienced through Christ. No longer subject to the infallible magisterium of a church, they were subject to Christ personally, and therefore free to develop doctrines and worship under the influence of the Holy Spirit. As they did this, however, they incorporated their doctrines and worship in denominations of their own. This happened so often that it looked as though Protestantism and disunity were inseparable. Certainly many Protestants were afraid it was, and all Catholics were sure it was.

Then about 1900, Protestants began to ask a question about themselves. They observed that despite their denominations they were all engaged in two forms of Christian obedience: witnessing to the world of God's love in Christ, and ministering to the earthly needs of men. What is more, Protestants observed that often they were doing these two things together, especially on the mission field, where they worked with each other in a great variety of ways. Looking at this situation, Protestants asked: "Why do we do this? Why, though our denominations differ somewhat in doctrine and worship, do we all do the same two things, and why do we do them together?"

Through the Bible, Protestants found the answer: they were one in Christ. They were doing the same things, and often together, because they were one in obedience to him through whom they met God. Through Christ they were one in the obedience that is Christian evangelism — the effort to bring all men to accept Christ. Through Christ they were one in the obedience which is Christian benevolence — the effort to heal the sick, feed the hungry, educate the ignorant, comfort the widow and the orphan.

At this point, Protestants heard a challenge to discover the full meaning of their oneness in Christ. They were one in the obediences of evangelism and benevolence. But what did oneness mean beyond that? What did it mean for further obedience? What did it mean for doctrines and worship? What did it mean for the existence of denominations?

The answer Protestants have given to that challenge was the ecumenical movement. The word " ecumenical " comes from the Greek word *oikoumenikos,* which refers to something encompassing or representing the whole world. Protestants, using the word, express their hope and prayer that the whole Christian world will join with them in learning how to know and express more fully the meaning of unity in Christ. They hope that the Christian world will join with them in answering, under God, the prayer Christ prayed when he met with his disciples during the night hours before his crucifixion: " I do not pray for these only, but also for those who are to believe in me through their word, that they may all be one " (John 17:20-21) .

Thus Protestants do not propose in the ecumenical movement a movement for Protestants only. It is a movement for all Christians — for Catholics of every variety as well as for Protestants of every variety. To the great joy of Protestants, some Catholic churches have come into it. Some Orthodox churches have come, churches from among those continuing on from the eleventh century when most of the world's Christians divided into Roman and Orthodox Catholic Churches. Some Old Catholic Churches have come, churches from among those which have maintained their separate existence since the first three or four Christian centuries. But the Roman Church remains outside.

It is a matter of great regret to Protestants that the Roman Catholic Church has not seen fit to enter the ecumenical movement. True, the Roman Church is impressed by the movement. An American Catholic theologian expressed both his and his church's feeling when he was quoted in the public press as saying that the ecumenical movement " is vital and effective, one of the best efforts the Protestant churches have ever made." Of course he might have added, " and also the Orthodox and Old Catholic

Churches." But, the Catholic Church believes, it cannot enter the ecumenical movement without contradicting and abandoning what it calls its own ecumenical movement, its open invitation to all non-Roman Christians to join the one true church, the Catholic Church. Still, the Roman Church has gone so far as to allow a few of its scholars to attend meetings of the World Council of Churches — of which more immediately — as unofficial observers. For their part, Protestants pray with all their hearts that the Roman Church will eventually come into the ecumenical movement to share with the other churches what it has to give of Christian insight and action.

The World Council of Churches is perhaps the most dramatic practical expression of the ecumenical movement. Planned just prior to World War II, it was formally constituted after the war in 1948 at a great assembly held in Amsterdam, in the Netherlands. Its membership now includes well over one hundred and fifty churches, Protestant denominations from around the world, and Orthodox and Old Catholic Churches. The World Council is not another church but an association of churches that, as its constitution states, "accept our Lord Jesus Christ as God and Savior," and member churches need not agree on exactly what that means. But in the World Council the churches have a joint enterprise through which they study together the meaning of unity in Christ, and through which they work together in projects of Christian benevolence such as relief work for the peoples impoverished by World War II.

The Orthodox Churches, to speak of them particularly, join fully in the work of the World Council even though, like the Roman Catholic Church, they believe themselves to comprise the one true church. But unlike the Roman Church, they do not believe that they deny what they hold to be their unique character by belonging to the World Council. As members of the World Council they unite in study and benevolence with their Christian brethren of the Protestant Churches. And as members of the World Council they help their Protestant brethren understand what they believe to be the true goal of any ecumenical movement, the coming of all non-Orthodox Christians into the Orthodox Churches.

There have been numerous practical expressions of the ecumenical movement in the United States. In 1908, Protestants organized a Federal Council of Churches, and as the years went by almost a thousand local and state councils of churches. Since 1930, there have been many unions of important Protestant denominations. Moreover, in 1950, the National Council of Churches was organized, combining the Federal Council and several co-operative Protestant agencies. American Orthodox and Old Catholic Churches have come into the National Council. Among other things, the Council encourages Bible study, publishes materials for missionary education, and studies the application of Christianity to modern social problems.

Working and studying together in the ecumenical movement, Protestants are coming increasingly to see that the Protestant understanding of Christian experience does not, after all, lead to the disunity of Christians; it leads to their unity. As was said earlier, formerly Protestant denominations justified their disunity by arguing their differences in doctrine and worship. But the ecumenical movement is bringing Protestants to a renewed appreciation of the meaning of their fundamental Christian experience; and that meaning is unity.

For Protestants, men become Christians through their personal encounter with God through the Bible. They do not become Christians through particular doctrines and types of worship; these follow from the personal encounter in an effort to express its meaning. Men become Christians through a personal encounter with God common to them all. And through it they do not become either theologians or liturgists in Christ — they become brothers in Christ. Their oneness with Christ is personal, and because their oneness with Christ is personal, their oneness with their fellow Christians is personal.

All Christians, therefore, in their very first Christian experience are united in Christ. What is more, so long as they renew their experience they can never be disunited. It is only when they allow that experience of personal encounter with God to wane that they become disunited; for then they begin to regard each other impersonally, that is, as theologians and liturgists of different doctrines and types of worship. This does not mean that they can give up differences in doctrine and worship. As long as men think and worship, doctrines and types of worship are inevitable; and as long as men live they will never think and do things in exactly the same way. But this it does mean: by constantly renewing the experience of personal encounter with God they can have such a powerful sense of oneness with each other that differences in doctrine and liturgy cannot separate them from each other. This is the Protestant experience of Christianity, personal encounter with God through the Bible; and it leads not to the disunity of Christians but to their unity.

A Last Word

This last word is a prayer.

Almighty and all-loving Father:
Thou hast drawn near to us in love through thy Son, our Lord Jesus Christ; and we praise and thank thee for all that means to us of goodness, and peace, and joy with thee and with our fellow men, now and for eternity.
Forgive thy Protestant servants who would follow thee through loyalty to Christ, every sinful disposition by which they fail to understand their Catholic brothers-in-Christ, and by which they fail to act as Christians ought to act toward their Catholic brothers-in-Christ.
Increase in both thy Protestant servants and thy Catholic servants who would follow thee through loyalty to Christ, the spirit and the wisdom of Christ, so that they may come to realize the limitations of their minds, grow in appreciation of the judgments of others, and increase together in the knowledge of thy will.
Come into the hearts of thy Protestant and Catholic servants with thy truth and thy power; despite the divisions among them, use them to accomplish thy design, and draw them together in Christian faith and work so that they may more effectively withstand the forces of evil.
And grant that this prayer be prayed in no selfish seeking after power or glory for either Protestantism or Catholicism, but in the righteous seeking of thy power and glory.
This prayer is made through the name of Jesus Christ, the Lord. Amen.